MEL BAY PRESENTS

# SONGS OF ENGLAND

## 100 Favourite English Songs

By Jerry Silverman

APR 29 1994

Glenview _____ Library
1930 Glenview Road
Glenview, Illinois

784.71942
MEL

# A Note From Jerry Silverman

English folk songs have a familiar ring to them. Hundreds upon hundreds of them have crossed the Atlantic. Some arrived with the earliest settlers in the 17th century; others with the Redcoats in the 18th century; still others with the sailors and fishermen of the 19th century; and finally the doughboys and G.I.s of two world wars have brought over the 20th century's contribution.

We know these lords and ladies of merrie England, these outlaws and lovers, these soldiers, sailors, and working people. From Maine to Georgia and points west, they have peopled our own folk-song tradition and literature. Old stories have been retold, old melodies borrowed, new characters have appeared in place of the old: Villikins' daughter Dinah became Betsy; Earl Tyrconnell became Jeff Davis; the dying sailor became the dying cowboy. . . .

If, as Winston Churchill said, Great Britain and the United States are divided by a common language, then we are most assuredly united by this other language — the language of song.

# The Cassette

I have recorded exerpts from each of the songs that should serve as a guide and help those who may have some difficulty transforming cold music notation into living music.

# Contents

# Lincolnshire Poacher

From the time of Richard II (1389) to 1831, no person might kill game unless qualified by estate or social standing. In 1831 the qualification by estate was abolished. The Night Poaching Laws of 1828 and 1844 specify: If the trespass is in search or pursuit of game or rabbits in the nighttime, the maximum penalty on first conviction is imprisonment with hard labour for not over three months; on a second, imprisonment &c., for not over six months. For a third offense the offender is liable to penal servitude (3–7 years). If three or more trespass together on land by night, and any of them is armed with firearms, bludgeon or other offensive weapon, they are liable to penal servitude of 3 to 14 years.

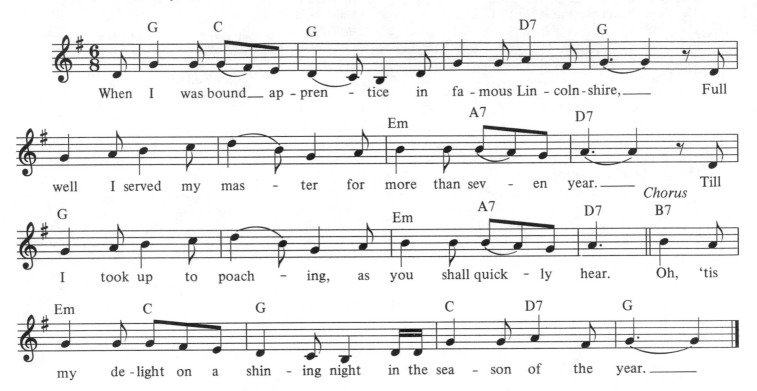

When I was bound apprentice in famous Lincolnshire, Full well I served my master for more than seven year. Till I took up to poaching, as you shall quickly hear. Oh, 'tis my delight on a shining night in the season of the year.

    G    C    G
As me and my companions
         D7  G
were setting of a snare,

'Twas when we spied the gamekeeper,
     Em    A7    D7
for him we did not care,
    G
For we can wrestle and fight, my boys,
     Em      A7  D7
and jump out anywhere. *Chorus*

    G    C    G
I threw him on my shoulder
          D7    G
and then we trudged home,

We took him to a neighbor's house
     Em    A7    D7
and sold him for a crown.
    G
We sold him for a crown, my boys,
     Em    A7    D7
but I did not tell you where. *Chorus*

    G    C    G
As me and my companions
         D7  G
were setting four or five,

And taking on 'em up again,
     Em    A7    D7
we caught a hare alive,
    G
We took a hare alive, my boys,
     Em    A7    D7
and through the woods did steer. *Chorus*

    G    C    G
Success to ev'ry gentleman
         D7  G
that lives in Lincolnshire,

Success to ev'ry poacher
     Em    A7    D7
that wants to sell a hare,
    G
Bad luck to ev'ry gamekeeper
     Em    A7    D7
that will not sell his deer. *Chorus*

# Old Maid's Song

John, Duke of Roxburghe (1740–1804) was a famous bibliophile. His library included three rare volumes of broadside ballads. This song was included in the Roxburghe Collection. It was reprinted in America in 1814 in *The Columbia Harmonist.*

Come a lands - man, a pins - man, a tin - ker or a tai - lor,_____ Fid - dler or a dan - cer, a plough - boy or a sai - lor;_____ Gen - tle - man, or poor - man, a fool or a wit - ty. Don't you let me die an old maid, But take me out of pit - y.

| G | Em | Am | D7 |
Oh, I had a sister Sally, was younger than I am,
| G | Em | A7 | D7 |
She had so many sweethearts, she had to deny them;
| G | G7 | C | Cm |
As for my own part I never had many,
| G | C G | C | D7 |
If you all knew my heart, I'd be thankful for any.

| G | Em | Am | D7 |
Oh, I had a sister Susan, was ugly and misshapen,
| G | Em | Am | D7 |
Before she was sixteen years old she was taken,
| G | G7 | C | Cm |
Before she was eighteen, a son and a daughter,
| G | C G | C | D7 |
Here am I six and forty and nary an offer.

| G | Em | Am | D7 |
Oh, I never will be scolding, I never will be jealous,
| G | Em | Am | D7 |
My husband shall have money to go to the alehouse,
| G | G7 | C | Cm |
While he's there a-spending, well, I'll be home a-saving,
| G | C G | C | D7 |
And I'll leave it to the world if I am not worth having.

# Scarborough Fair

William Chappell, in his 1840 volume *Old English Popular Music,* remarks, concerning this song: "The present copy . . . used to be sung by a ballad singer in Whitby streets twenty or thirty years ago, and is still remembered in the district."

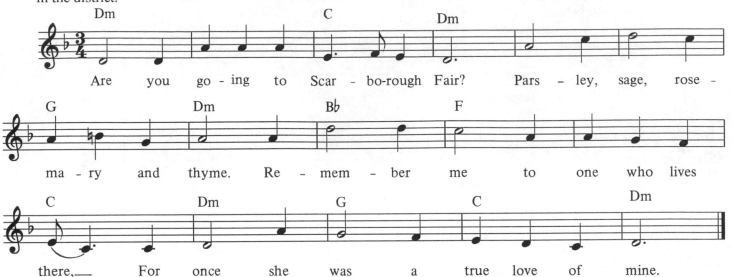

Are you go-ing to Scar-bo-rough Fair? Pars – ley, sage, rose – ma-ry and thyme. Re – mem – ber me to one who lives there,— For once she was a true love of mine.

Dm          C  Dm
Tell her to make me a cambric shirt.
  F  Dm   G    Dm
Parsley, sage, rosemary and thyme.
Bb   F              C
Without any seam or fine needlework.
    Dm   G  C     Dm
And then she'll be a true love of mine.

Dm           C  Dm
Tell her to wash it in yonder dry well.
  F  Dm   G    Dm
Parsley, sage, rosemary and thyme.
  Bb      F           C
Where water ne'er sprung, nor drop of rain fell.
    Dm   G  C     Dm
And then she'll be a true love of mine.

Dm          C  Dm
Tell her to dry it on yonder thorn.
  F  Dm   G     Dm
Parsley, sage, rosemary and thyme.
  Bb     F           C
Which never bore blossom since Adam was born.
    Dm   G  C    Dm
And then she'll be a true love of mine.

Dm           C  Dm
Will you find me an acre of land.
  F  Dm   G    Dm
Parsley, sage, rosemary and thyme.
  Bb     F          C
Between the sea foam and the sea sand.
    Dm G  C    Dm
Or never be a true love of mine.

Dm           C  Dm
Will you plough it with a lamb's horn.
  F  Dm   G    Dm
Parsley, sage, rosemary and thyme.
  Bb     F           C
And sow it all over with one peppercorn,
    Dm G  C    Dm
Or never be a true love of mine.

Dm           C  Dm
Will you reap it with sickle of leather.
  F  Dm   G    Dm
Parsley, sage, rosemary and thyme.
  Bb     F           C
And tie it all up with a peacock's feather.
    Dm G  C     Dm
Or never be a true love of mine.

          Dm           C        Dm
When you've done and finished your work.
       F  Dm   G     Dm
Parsley, sage, rosemary and thyme.
   Bb     F             C
Then come to me for your cambric shirt.
      Dm    G  C     Dm
And you shall be a true love of mine.

# The Butcher Boy

She went up - stairs_____ to_ make her bed,_____

And not a word_____ to her moth – er said._____

Her moth – er she_____ went_ up - stairs too,_____

Say ing, "Daugh-ter, oh daugh-ter, _____ what_ trou - bles you?"_____

Em
"Oh mother, oh mother, I cannot tell,
    G          Em
That butcher boy I love so well.

He courted me my life away,
    G          Em
And now at home he will not stay.

Em
"There is a place in London Town,
    G          Em
To where he goes and sits him down.

He takes that strange girl on his knee,
    G          Em
And tells her what he won't tell me."

Em
Her father, he came home from work,
        G          Em
Saying, "Where is daughter, she seems so hurt?"

He went upstairs to give her hope,
        G          Em
And found her hanging from a rope.

Em
He took his knife and cut her down,
    G          Em
And in her bosom these words he found:

"Go dig my grave both wide and deep,
        G          Em
Place a marble slab at my head and feet.

*Sung to measures 9–16*
Em
And over my coffin place a snow-white dove,
    G          Em
To warn the world I died of love."

# Blow the Candles Out

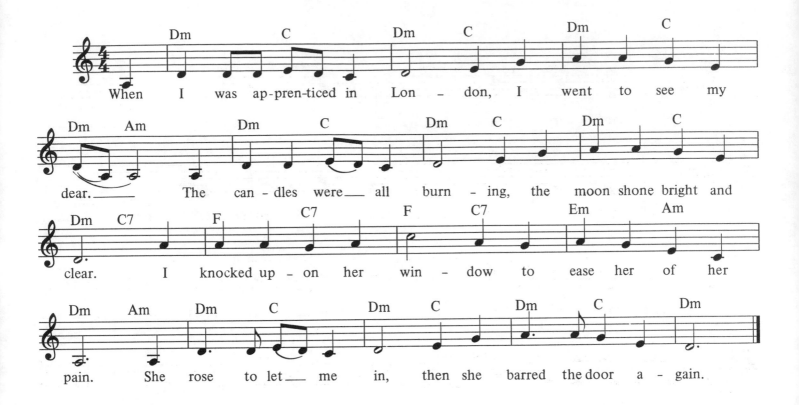

When I was ap-pren-ticed in Lon – don, I went to see my dear. ___ The can-dles were ___ all burn – ing, the moon shone bright and clear. I knocked up – on her win – dow to ease her of her pain. She rose to let ___ me in, then she barred the door a – gain.

Dm    C  Dm C    Dm  C  Dm Am
I like your well behaviour and thus I often say,
    Dm  C   Dm C    Dm   C  Dm C7
I cannot rest contented whilst you are far away.
      F       C7   F C7    Em  Am  Dm Am
The roads they are so muddy, we cannot gang about,
    Dm  C   Dm C    Dm   C   Dm
So roll me in your arms, love, and blow the candles out.

      Dm C    Dm C  Dm   C   Dm Am
Your father and your mother in yonder room do lie,
    Dm  C  Dm C    Dm   C    Dm C7
A-huggin' one another, so why not you and I?
     F    C7 F C7    Em Am   Dm Am
A-huggin' one another without fear or doubt,
    Dm  C   Dm C    Dm   C   Dm
So roll me in your arms, love, and blow the candles out.

      Dm  C   Dm   C    Dm   C Dm Am
And if you prove successful, love, pray name it after me,
    Dm C   Dm   C    Dm C    Dm C7
Keep it neat and kiss it sweet, and daff it on your knee,
     F    C7    F C7    Em  Am  Dm Am
When my three years are ended, my time it will be out,
    Dm  C    Dm  C   Dm    C   Dm
Then I will double my indebtedness by blowing the candles out.

# The Foggy Foggy Dew

The meaning of the expression "foggy dew" has puzzled generations of folkorists. "Chastity," "virginity," and "maidenhead" have all been suggested, in addition to "the black plague" (as a result of an English mispronunciation of the Irish "orocedhu"—meaning "dark"). Of course, the dark could just as well be a reference to the dark of night and its attendant foggy, foggy dew.

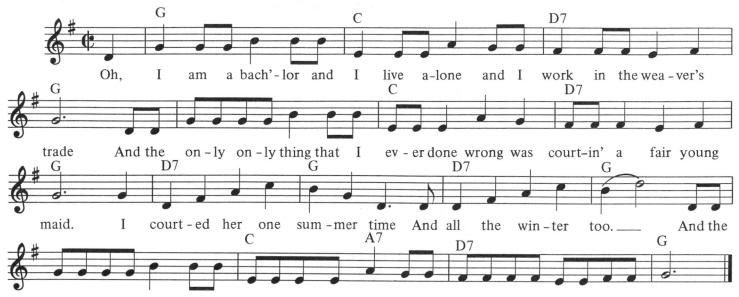

Oh, I am a bach'-lor and I live a-lone and I work in the wea-ver's trade And the on-ly on-ly thing that I ev-er done wrong was court-in' a fair young maid. I court-ed her one sum-mer time And all the win-ter too.___ And the on-ly on-ly thing that I nev-er should 'ave done was to save her from the fog-gy fog-gy dew.

G        C
I got that tired a living alone,
D7       G
I says to her one day;
           C
"I've a nice little crib in my old shack
D7       G
Where you might safely lay;
    D7     G
You'll be all right in the summer time
    D7      G
And in the winter, too,
             C      A7
And you'll lay right warm and take no harm,
D7         G
Away from the foggy, foggy dew."

G        C
"I don't think much o' this old shack
D7       G
And I shall lonely be;
           C
With only that poor old Cyprus cat
D7       G
To keep me company.
       D7     G
There's a cricket singing on the hearth,
    D7      G
And what can that thing do
            C     A7
If the night turn raw and the fire won't draw
    D7          G
To save me from the foggy, foggy dew."

G        C
One night she come to my bedside,
    D7     G
Time I laid fast asleep,
           C
She puts her head down on my bed
D7       G
And she starts in to weep;
    D7       G
She yelled and cried, she well near died,
    D7      G
She say, "What shall I do?"
            C      A7
So I hauled her into bed and I covered up her head
D7          G
To save her from the foggy, foggy dew.

          G        C
Says I, "My dear, lay close to me
    D7      G
And wipe away them tears,"
           C
Then I hauled her shift up over her head
     D7      G
And I wrapped it 'round her ears,
    D7      G
We was all right in the winter time,
    D7      G
And in the summer, too;
             C      A7
And I held her tight that live-long night,
D7          G
To save her from the foggy, foggy dew.

         G        C
"Now lay you still, you silly young fool,
    D7      G
And don't you feel afraid.
           C
For if you want to work with me,
    D7      G
You got to learn your trade."
D7         G
I learned her all that summer time,
    D7      G
And all the winter, too,
            C      A7
And truth to tell she learned that well;
    D7          G
She saved us from the foggy, foggy dew.

         G        C
One night I laid there good as gold
    D7      G
And then she say to me,
           C
"I got a pain without my back
    D7      G
Where no pain ought to be.
    D7      G
I was all right in the summer time,
    D7      G
And in the winter, too,
             C      A7
But I've took some ill or a kind of a chill
D7          G
From laying in the foggy, foggy dew."

         G        C
One night she start to moan and cry,
    D7      G
Says I, "What's up with you?"
           C
She say, "I never should've been this way,
    D7      G
If that hadn't 've been for you."
D7         G
I got my boots and trousers on,
D7         G
I got my neighbor, too,
            C      A7
But do what we would, we couldn't do no good,
    D7          G
And she died in the foggy, foggy dew.

         G          C
So I am a bachelor, I live with my son,
    D7       G
And we work in the weavin' trade;
           C
And every time I look in his face I can see
    D7          G
The eyes of that fair young maid:
    D7       G
It reminds me of the summer time,
    D7       G
And of the winter, too,
            C      A7
And the many, many nights she laid in my arms,
    D7          G
To save her from the foggy, foggy dew.

# The Passionate Shepherd to His Love

Christopher Marlowe (1564–1593) wrote this in 1599. Algernon Charles Swinburne, writing in the 1911 edition of *The Encyclopedia Britannica,* called it: "One of the most faultless lyrics and one of the loveliest fragments in the whole range of descriptive and fanciful poetry. . . . His *Passionate Shepherd* remains unrivalled in its way — a way of pure fantasy and radiant melody without break or lapse."

|  |  |  |
|---|---|---|
| Em | Am B7 | Em |
| And we will sit upon the rocks, | | A gown made of the finest wool |
| Em D G | | Em D G |
| And see the shepherds feed their flocks | | Which from our pretty lambs we pull; |
| C A7 D | | C A7 D |
| By shallow rivers, to whose falls | | Fair-lined slippers for the cold, |
| B7 Em Am Em B7 Em | | B7 Em Am Em B7 Em |
| Melodious birds sing madrigals. | | With buckles of the purest gold; |
| | | |
| Em Am B7 | | Em Am B7 |
| And I will make thee beds of roses | | A belt of straw and ivy buds |
| Em D G | | Em D G |
| And a thousand fragrant posies; | | With coral clasps and amber studs – |
| C A7 D | | C A7 D |
| A cap of flowers, and a kirtle | | And if these pleasures may thee move, |
| B7 Em Am Em B7 Em | | B7 Em Am Em B7 Em |
| Embroidered all with leaves of myrtle; | | Come live with me and be my Love. |

              Em            Am            B7
The shepherd swains shall dance and sing
              Em            D         G
For thy delight each May morning –
                C          A7         D
If these delights thy mind may move,
     B7     Em          Am      Em B7 Em
Then live with me and be my Love.

# Lord Thomas and Fair Ellender

A version of this appears in a broadside entitled *A Tragical Ballad of the Unfortunate Loves of Lord Thomas and Fair Eleanor, circa* 1740. In 1723, it appeared in *Old Ballads,* bespeaking a still earlier origin.

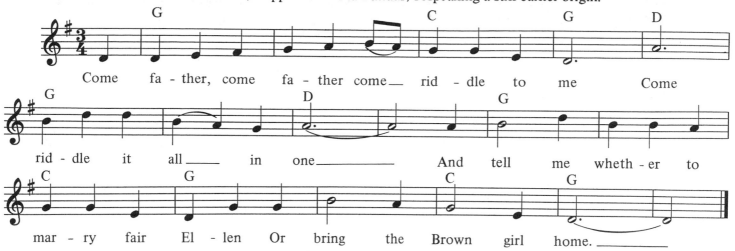

Come fa - ther, come fa - ther come__ rid - dle to me Come rid - dle it all ____ in one_____ And tell me wheth - er to mar - ry fair El - len Or bring the Brown girl home. _____

```
        G               C              G
The Brown girl she has house and land,
D       G             D
Fair Ellender she has none,
        G               C           G
And there I charge you with the blessing
              C         G
To bring the Brown girl home.

        G                C           G
He got on his horse and he rode and he rode.
D       G               D
He rode 'til he came to the home,
        G                C         G
And no one so ready as Fair Ellen herself
              C         G
To rise and bid him in.

              G                     C       G
What news have you brought unto me, Lord Thomas?
D       G                       D
What news have you brought unto me?
              G            C    G
I've come to ask you to my wedding,
              C         G
A sorrowful wedding to be.

        G                        C    G
Oh mother, oh mother, would you go or stay?
D       G             D
Fair Child, do as you please,
        G                    C        G
I'm afraid if you go you'll never return
              C         G
To see your mother any more.

        G                    C       G
She turned around and dressed in white,
D       G                 D
Her sisters dressed in green,
        G                   C      G
And every town that they rode through
              C         G
Took her to be some queen.
```

```
        G                     C           G
They rode and they rode 'til they came to the hall,
D       G                 D
She pulled on the bell and it rang,
        G                          C        G
And no one so ready as Lord Thomas himself
              C         G
To rise and bid them in.

        G                    C         G
And taking her by her lily-white hand,
D       G                   D
And leading her through the hall,
              G               C      G
Saying, "Fifty gay ladies are here today,
              C         G
But here is the flower of all."

        G                 C       G
Lord Thomas he was standing by,
D       G                 D
With knife ground keen and sharp.
        G                      C      G
Between the long ribs and the short,
              C         G
He pierced his own bride's heart.

        G                  C        G
The Brown girl she was standing by,
D       G                 D
With knife ground keen and sharp.
        G                      C      G
Between the long ribs and the short,
              C         G
She pierced fair Ellender's heart.

        G                        C        G
Then placing the handle against the wall,
D       G                 D
The point against his breast,
              G                         C           G
Saying, "This is the ending of three true lovers,
              C         G
God sends them all to rest."
```

```
              G                 C       G
Oh father, oh father, go dig my grave,
D       G             D
Go dig it wide and deep,
              G                 C      G
And place fair Ellender in my arms,
              C         G
And the Brown girl at my feet.
```

# The Willow Song

In Act IV, Scene III, of Shakespeare's *Othello,* Desdemona sings this song just prior to her death at Othello's hands. In Verdi's opera *Otello* it appears as a magnificent aria, sung to the composer's original music.

A poor soul sat sigh - ing by a syc - a - more tree, Sing
oh, the green__ Wil - low, with his hand on his bos - om And his
head up - on his knee. Sing wil - low, wil - low, wil - low, wil - low, Sing
wil - low, wil - low, wil - low, wil - low, my gar - land shall be. Sing
oh, the green wil - low, Wil - low, wil - low, wil - low, Sing
oh, the green__ wil - low my gar - land shall be.

| | | | | | |
|---|---|---|---|---|---|
| Em | B7 Em | G | D7 G | | |
He sighed in his singing and made a great moan,

Em
Sing, oh, the green willow.

G   D7 G    Am      B7
I am dead to all pleasure, my true love she is gone. *Chorus*

Em        B7 Em        G       D7 G
The mute bird sat by him, was made tame by his moans,

Em
Sing, oh, the green willow.

G      D7 G           Am      B7
The true tears fell from him would have melted the stones.

Em   B7 Em      G    D7 G
Let Love no more boast her in palace nor bower,

Em
Sing, oh, the green willow.

G    D7 G    Am     B7
It buds but it blasteth, ere it be a flower.  *Chorus*

Em       B7 Em  G      D7 G
Thou fair and more false, I died with thy wound,

Em
Sing, oh, the green willow.

G      D7 G        Am          B7
Thou hast lost the truest lover that goes upon the ground.

```
    Em    B7 Em      G        D7 G
Come all you forsaken and mourn you with me;
     Em
Sing, oh, the green willow.
     G    D7 G              Am      B7
Who speaks of a false love, mine's falser than she.   *Chorus*
```

```
    Em    B7 Em      G       D7 G
Let nobody chide her, frowns I approve,
     Em
Sing, oh, the green willow.
     G    D7 G              Am      B7
She was born to be false and I to die of love.   *Chorus*
```

```
         Em   B7 Em     G   D7 G
Take this for my farewell and latest adieu,
         Em
Sing, oh, the green willow.
      G    D7 G          Am      B7
Write this on my tomb, that in love I was true.   *Chorus*
```

# How Should I Your True Love Know

QUEEN.  To my sick soul, a sin's true nature is,
Each toy seems prologue to some great amiss.
So full of artless jealousy is guilt,
It spills itself in fearing to be spilt.

*Enter* OPHELIA *[distracted]*

OPHELIA. Where is the beauteous majesty of Denmark?
QUEEN. How now, Ophelia!
OPHELIA. *(sings)* How should I your true love know . . .
QUEEN. Alas, sweet lady, what imports this song?
OPHELIA. Say you?  Nay, pray you mark.

*(Hamlet.* Act IV, Scene V)

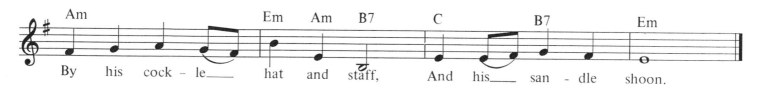

```
Em              B7 A♯°B7
He is dead and gone, lady,
 Em  D7    G
He is dead and gone.
  Am        Em   Am B7
At his head a grass-green turf,
 C   B7   Em
At his head a stone.
```

```
  Em              B7 A♯°  B7
White his shroud as the mountain snow,
  Em    D7       G
Larded with sweet flow'rs.
   Am            Em   Am B7
Which bewept to the grave did go,
  C  B7      Em
With true love show'rs.
```

13

# Drink to Me Only with Thine Eyes

In his 1616 play *Volpone,* Ben Jonson (1573–1637) has Volpone sing this "Song to Celia" (as it is entitled in the play) in Act III.

# Edward

A variant of the traditional Child #13 ballad. In some cases Edward confesses to his mother that he has killed his brother, in others it is his father.

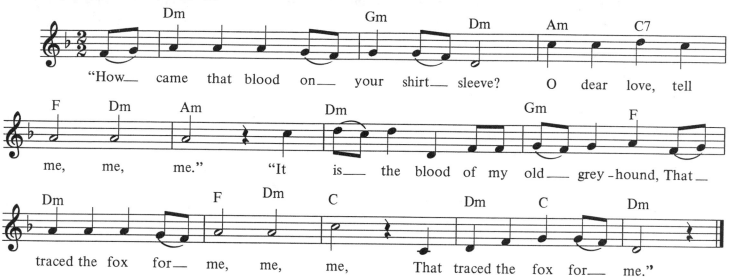

"How— came that blood on— your shirt— sleeve? O dear love, tell me, me, me." "It is— the blood of my old— grey-hound, That— traced the fox for— me, me, me, That traced the fox for— me."

Dm      Gm  Dm
"It does look too pale for the old greyhound,
Am  C7   F Dm Am
O dear love, tell me, me me.
Dm      Gm     F
It does look too pale for the old greyhound,
Dm     F Dm C
That traced the fox for thee, thee, thee,
Dm  C  Dm
That traced the fox for thee."

Dm      Gm  Dm
"How came that blood on your shirt sleeve?
Am  C7   F Dm Am
O dear love, tell me, me, me."
Dm      Gm     F
"It is the blood of my old grey mare,
Dm     F Dm C
That ploughed the field for me, me, me,
Dm  C  Dm
That ploughed the field for me."

Dm      Gm  Dm
"It does look too pale for the old grey mare,
Am  C7   F Dm Am
O dear son, tell me, me, me.
Dm      Gm     F
It does look too pale for the old grey mare,
Dm     F Dm C
That ploughed the field for thee, thee, thee,
Dm  C  Dm
That ploughed the field for thee."

Dm      Gm    Dm
"How came this blood on your shirt sleeve?
Am  C7   F Dm Am
O dear love, tell me, me, me."
Dm      Gm     F
"It is the blood of my brother-in-law,
Dm     F Dm C
That went away with me, me, me,
Dm  C  Dm
That went away with me."

Dm      Gm Dm
"And what did you fall out about?
Am  C7   F Dm Am
O dear love, tell me, me, me."
Dm      Gm     F
"About a little bit of bush
Dm          F  Dm C
That never would-a growed to a tree, tree, tree,
Dm     C  F
That never would-a growed to a tree."

Dm      Gm  Dm
"And it's what will you do now, my son?
Am  C7   F Dm Am
O dear love, tell me, me, me!"
Dm      Gm     F
"I'll set my foot on yonder ship,
Dm     F Dm C
And sail across the sea, sea, sea,
Dm C  Dm
And sail across the sea."

Dm      Gm  Dm
"And it's when will you come back again?
Am  C7   F Dm Am
O dear love, tell me, me, me!"
Dm      Gm     F
"When the sun sets into yonder sycamore tree,
Dm     F Dm C
And that will never be, be, be,
Dm    C Dm
And that will never be."

# The Cruel Mother

Variants of "The Cruel Mother" (Child #20) are found in America from Maine to Georgia — remnants of the migrations of the 17th century.

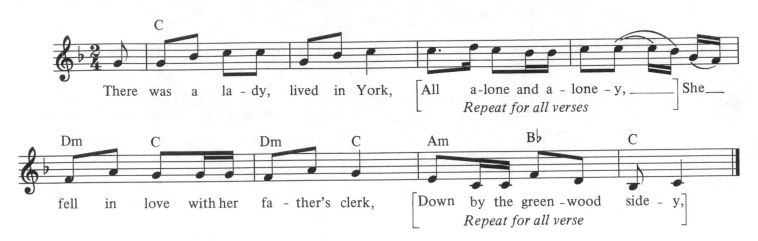

She loved him up, she loved him down. . .
Dm    C   Dm    C
She loved him till he filled her arms. . .

C
She leaned her back against an oak. . .
Dm  C    Dm    C
First it bent and then it broke. . .

C
She leaned her back against a thorn. . .
Dm    C   Dm     C
And there she had two fine babies born. . .

C
She pulléd down her yellow hair. . .
Dm    C     Dm    C
She bound it around their feet and hands. . .

C
She pulléd out a wee penknife. . .
Dm      C   Dm  C
Stabbed those two babes to the heart. . .

C
She laid them under a marble stone. . .
Dm     C Dm     C
Then she turned as a fair maid home. . .

C
One day was sitting in her father's hall. . .
Dm    C     Dm    C
She saw two babes come playing at ball. . .

C
Babes, oh, babes, if you was nine. . .
Dm    C   Dm   C
I'd dress you up in scarlet fine. . .

C
Mother, oh, mother, it's we was yours. . .
Dm C      Dm      C
Scarlet fine was our own heart's blood. . .

C
You wiped your penknife on your shoe. . .
Dm     C    Dm C
The more you wiped, more red it grew. . .

C
You laid us under a marble stone. . .
Dm   C  Dm     C
Now you sit as a fair maid home. . .

C
Babes, oh, babes, it's Heaven for you. . .
Dm     C    Dm   C
Mother, oh, mother, it's Hell for you. . .

# It Was a Lover and His Lass

Thomas Morley (1557–1603) composed this song, and Shakespeare used it in Act V, Scene III, of *As You Like It*. It first appears in Morley's *First Booke of Ayres, or Little Short Songs, to sing and play to the Lute* (1600).

Between the acres of the rye,
With a hey and a ho and a hey nonni no,
With a hey nonni nonni no,
These pretty country folk would lie.    *Chorus*

And therefore at the present time,
With a hey and a ho and a hey nonni no,
With a hey nonni nonni no,
For love is crowned with the prime.    *Chorus*

17

# Cock Robin

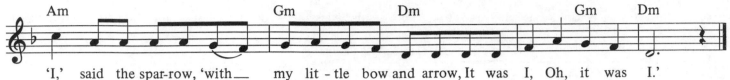

Dm
Who caught his blood - o?
Gm
Who caught his blood- o?
Am
"I," said the fish,
        Gm      Dm
"With my little silver dish,
        Gm  Dm
It was I, oh, it was I."

Dm
Who sewed his shroud - o?
 Gm        Dm
Who sewed his shroud - o?
 Am
"I," said the eagle,
        Gm       Dm
"With my little thread and needle,
        Gm  Dm
It was I, oh, it was I."

 Dm
Who made the coffin?
 Gm        Dm
Who made the coffin?
 Am
"I," said the snipe,
        Gm       Dm
"With my little pocket knife,
        Gm  Dm
It was I, oh, it was I."

Dm
Who dug his grave - o?
Gm        Dm
Who dug his grave - o?
 Am
"I," said the owl,
        Gm       Dm
"With my little wooden shovel,
        Gm  Dm
It was I, oh, it was I."

 Dm
Who lowered him down - o?
 Gm        Dm
Who lowered him down - o?
 Am
"I," said the crane,
        Gm       Dm
"With my little golden chain,
        Gm  Dm
It was I, oh, it was I."

Dm
Who sang the preachment?
 Gm        Dm
Who sang the preachment?
 Am
"I," sang the rook,
        Gm       Dm
"With my little holy book,
        C  Dm
It was I, oh, it was I."

# Johnson's Ale

Five jol-ly rogues of a feath-er___ walked o'er the hill to – geth-er [And who could be so bold as to join our jov-i-al crew?___] And they *repeat for every verse* called for their pots of beer and their sher-ry to help them o'er the hills so mer-ry, To help them o'er the hills so mer-ry, When *Chorus* John-son's ale was new, my boys, When John-son's ale was new.

G
Now the first to come in was the Dyer,
D7              G
And he sat down by the fire...
G
And the landlady told him straight to his face
            D
That the chimney corner was his own place,
C                    G
And there he could sit and dye his old face. *Chorus*

G
The next to come in was the hatter,
        D7          G
And no man could be fatter...
G
And he threw his big hat down on the ground;
D
He swore all men should stand a-crowned,
C                        G
For that would pay for the drinks all around. *Chorus*

G
The next to come in was the mason;
        D7          G
His hammer it needed a facing...
G
And he threw his hammer against the wall,
D
He swore all cellars and chimneys should fall,
C                            G
For that would give work to the masons all. *Chorus*

G
The next to come in was the sailor,
            D7          G
With his marlin spike and his heaver...
G
And he told the landlord straight to his face
D
He thought it was time to splice the main brace,
C                    G
With his tarpaulin hat he was a hard case. *Chorus*

G
Now the last to come in was the soldier,
        D7          G
With his flintlock on his shoulder...
G
And the landlady's daughter she came in,
D
And he kissed her o'er from cheek to chin,
C                    G
Then the pots of beer come a-rolling in. *Chorus*

19

# On Mondays I Never Go to Work

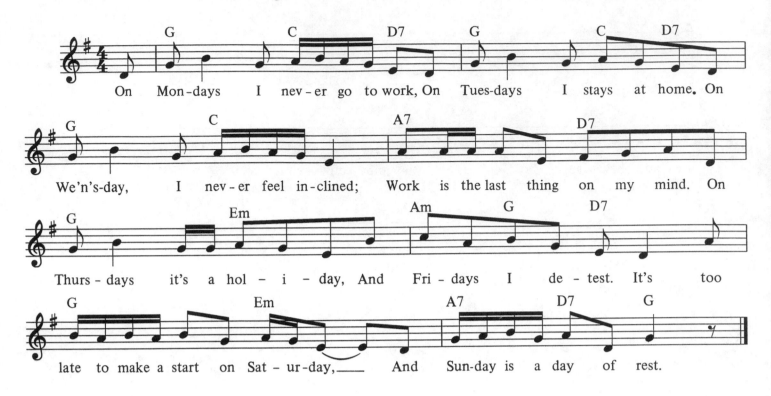

On Mon-days I nev-er go to work, On Tues-days I stays at home. On We'n's-day, I nev-er feel in-clined; Work is the last thing on my mind. On Thurs-days it's a hol-i-day, And Fri-days I de-test. It's too late to make a start on Sat-ur-day,___ And Sun-day is a day of rest.

# The Maid on the Shore

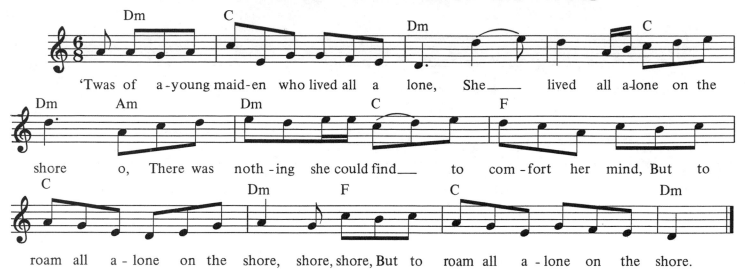

'Twas of a-young maid-en who lived all a lone, She lived all a-lone on the shore o, There was noth-ing she could find to com-fort her mind, But to roam all a-lone on the shore, shore, shore, But to roam all a-lone on the shore.

|   |   |   |
|---|---|---|
| Dm | C | Dm |

'Twas of a young captain who sailed the salt sea,
C       Dm Am
Let the wind blow high or low - o.
Dm       C       F
"I will die, I will die," the young captain did cry,
C       Dm       F
"If I don't get that maid on the shore, shore, shore,
C       Dm
If I don't get that maid on the shore."

Dm       C       Dm
"I have lots of silver, I have lots of gold.
C       Dm Am
I have lots of costly wear - o.
Dm       C       F
I'll divide, I'll divide with my jolly ship's crew,
Dm       F
If they'll row me that maid from the shore, shore, shore,
C       Dm
If they'll row me that maid from the shore."

Dm       C       Dm
After long persuadence they got her on board,
C       Dm Am
Let the wind blow high or low - o,
Dm       C       F
Where he placed her on a chair in his cabin below,
C       Dm       F
"Here's adieu to all sorrows and care, care, care,
C       Dm
Here's adieu to all sorrows and care."

Dm       C       Dm
Where he placed her on a chair in his cabin below,
C       Dm Am
Let the winds blow high or low - o,
Dm       C       F
She sung charming and sweet, she sung neat and complete,
C       Dm       F
She sung captain and sailors to sleep, sleep, sleep,
C       Dm
She sung captain and sailors to sleep.

Dm       C       Dm
She robbed him of silver, she robbed him of gold,
C       Dm Am
She robbed him of costly wear - o,
Dm       F
And she stole his broadsword, instead of an oar,
Dm       F
And she paddled her way to the shore, shore, shore,
C       Dm
And she paddled her way to the shore,

Dm       C       Dm
"My men must be crazy, my men must be mad,
C       Dm Am
My men must be deep in despair - o,
Dm       C       F
To let her go 'way, with her beauty so gay,
C       Dm       F
And paddle her way to the shore, shore, shore,
C       Dm
And paddle her way to the shore."

Dm       C       Dm
"Your men was not crazy, your men was not mad,
C       Dm Am
Your men was not deep in despair - o,
Dm       C       F
I deluded the sailors as well as yourself,
C       Dm       F
I'm a maiden again on the shore, shore, shore,
C       Dm
I'm a maiden again on the shore."

# Lady of Carlisle

Down in Car - lisle____ there lived a la - dy,____ Be -ing most beau - ti -ful and gay. ____ She was de -ter-mined ____ to live a la - dy, No man on earth could her be - tray.

G    Dm
Unless it were a man of honor,
C     G
A man of honor and high degree;
         Dm
And then approached two loving soldiers,
G   F  G
This fair lady for to see.

G    Dm
One being a brave lieutenant,
C     G
A brave lieutenant and a man of war;
        Dm
The other being a brave sea captain,
G   F  G
Captain of the ship that come from far.

G     Dm
Then up spoke this fair young lady,
C     G
Saying, "I can't be but one man's bride,
         Dm
But if you'll come back tomorrow morning,
G   F  G
On this case we will decide."

G    Dm
She ordered her a span of horses,
C    G
A span of horses at her command;
        Dm
And down the road these three did travel,
G   F  G
Till they come to the lions' den.

G     Dm
There she stopped and there she halted,
C     G
These two soldiers stood gazing around;
       Dm
And for the space of half an hour,
G   F  G
This young lady lies speechless on the ground.

G    Dm
And when she did recover,
C     G
Threw her fan down in the lions' den;
        Dm
Saying, "Which of you to gain a lady
G   F  G
Will return her fan again?"

G    Dm
Then up spoke the brave lieutenant,
C     G
Raised his voice both loud and clear,
          Dm
Saying, "You know I am a dear lover of women,
G   F  G
But I will not give my life for love."

G    Dm
Then up spoke this brave sea captain,
C     G
He raised his voice both loud and high,
          Dm
Saying, "You know I am a dear lover of women,
G   F  G
I will return her fan or die."

G    Dm
Down in the lions' den, he boldly entered,
C     G
The lions being both wild and fierce;
       Dm
He marched around and in among them,
G   F  G
Safely returned her fan again.

         Dm
And when she saw her true lover coming,
C     G
Seeing no harm had been done to him,
        Dm
She threw herself against his bosom,
G   F  G
Saying, "Here is the prize that you have won."

# Lady Margaret

La-dy Mar-ga-ret sit-tin' in her high hall door, comb ing her long yel low hair. She
saw sweet Wil-liam and his new made — bride, rid-in' from the church so near.

Em            D
Well, she throwed down her ivory comb,
Em            D
Throwed back her long yellow hair.
Bm            D
Said, "I'll go down to bid him farewell,
            Em
And never more go there."

Em            D
It was all lately in the night,
Em            D
When they were fast asleep,
Bm            D
Little Margaret appeared all dressed in white,
            Em
Standin' at their bed feet.

Em            D
"How do you like your pillow?" says she,
Em            D
"How do you like your sheet?
Bm            D
And how do you like that gay young bride
            Em
Lyin' in your arms asleep?"

Em            D
"Very well do I like my pillow," says he,
Em            D
"Very well do I like my sheet.
Bm            D
Better do I like that fair young lady,
            Em
Standin' at my bed feet."

Em            D
Well, once he kissed her lily-white hand,
Em            D
Twice he kissed her cheek,
Bm            D
Three times he kissed her cold, corpsey lips,
            Em
And fell in her arms asleep.

Em            D
Is little Margaret in her room,
Em            D
Or is she in the hall?
Bm            D
No, little Margaret's in her cold black coffin,
            Em
With her pale face to the wall.

# Lord Bateman

It is quite probable that the hero of this epic ballad was Gilbert áBecket, father of Saint Thomas áBecket of Canterbury, who in the early times of the Crusades was captured, released, and followed to London by the lady. She is said to have known no more than two words of English: "Gilbert" and "London," and to have cried the first through London streets until she found her lover. Fanciful as the legend appears, it is supported by the fact that every one of the many ballads known on the subject gives the name of the knight as a greater or lesser corruption of "Becket" ("Young Bekie," "Lord Beichan," "Lord Bateman," etc.).

Am          Em
He sailèd east and sailèd west,
Am       D Am    G
Until he came to fair Turkey,
C      Dm      Em
Where he was taken and put in prison,
Am          Em    Am
Until his life was quite weary.

Am            Em
And in this prison there grew a tree,
Am       D Am       G
It grew so stout and it grew so strong,
C      Dm      Em
Where he was chained by the middle,
Am          Em    Am
Until his life was almost gone.

Am          Em
The Turk he had an only daughter,
Am       D       Am      G
The fairest creature ever my eyes did see;
C      Dm      Em
She stole the keys of her father's prison,
Am          Em    Am
And swore Lord Bateman she would set free!

Am            Em
"Have you got houses, have you got lands?
Am       D Am    G
Or does Northumberland belong to thee?
C      Dm      Em
What would you give to the fair young lady,
Am          Em    Am
That out of prison would set you free?"

Am            Em
"I have got houses, I have got lands,
Am            D Am    G
And half Northumberland belongs to me;
C      Dm      Em
I'll give it all to the fair young lady,
Am          Em    Am
That out of prison would set me free."

Am          Em
Oh, then she took him to her father's palace,
Am       D Am       G
And gave to him the best of wine,
C      Dm      Em
And every health she drank unto him,
Am          Em      Am
"I wish, Lord Bateman, that you were mine."

Am            Em
"Now, for seven long years, I'll make a vow,
Am       D    Am   G
For seven long years, and keep it strong,
C      Dm      Em
If you will wed no other woman,
Am          Em  Am
That I will wed no other man."

Am            Em
Oh, then she took him to her father's harbour,
Am       D Am    G
And gave to him a ship of fame;
C      Dm      Em
"Farewell, farewell, my dear Lord Bateman,
Am          Em  Am
I'm afraid I shall never see you again."

Am     Em
Now, seven long years were gone and past,
  Am    D Am G
And fourteen long days well known to me,
 C  Dm Em
She packed up her gay clothing,
  Am    Em  Am
And Lord Bateman she would go see.

  Am    Em
And then she came to Lord Bateman's castle,
  Am   D Am G
So boldly now she rang the bell;
   C  Dm  Em
"Who's there?" cried the young porter,
   Am    Em Am
"Who's there now come unto me tell?"

  Am   Em
"Oh, is this Lord Bateman's castle,
  Am   D Am G
And is his Lordship here within?"
 C  Dm   Em
"O yes, O yes," cried the proud young porter,
   Am  Em  Am
He's just taking his young bride in."

  Am    Em
"Oh, then tell him to send me a slice of bread,
   Am  D Am G
And a bottle of the best wine;
  C  Dm  Em
And not forgetting the fair young lady,
   Am    Em Am
That did release him when close confined."

Am      Em
Away, away, went that proud young porter,
 Am   D Am   G
Away, away, and away went he,
C  Dm    Em
Until he came to Lord Bateman's door,
 Am    Em  Am
Down on his bended knees fell he.

   Am     Em
"What news, what news, my young porter,
   Am    D  Am G
What news have you brought unto me?"
   C  Dm  Em
"There is the fairest of all young ladies,
   Am   Em  Am
That ever my two eyes did see.

  Am     Em
"She has got rings on every finger,
   Am    D Am   G
And round one of them she has got three;
  C  Dm    Em
And such gay gold hanging round her middle,
     Am    Em  Am
That would buy Northumberland for thee.

    Am    Em
"She tells you to send her a slice of bread,
   Am  D Am G
And a bottle of the best wine;
  C  Dm   Em
And not forgetting the fair young lady,
   Am    Em   Am
That did release you when close confined."

    Am    Em
Lord Bateman then in a passion flew,
    Am   D Am  G
And broke his sword in splinters three,
   C  Dm   Em
Saying, "I will give all my father's riches,
   Am   Em   Am
If that Sophia has crossed the sea."

Am      Em
Then up spoke this bride's young mother,
   Am   D Am   G
Who never was heard to speak so free,
   C  Dm  Em
"You'll not forget my only daughter,
   Am   Em  Am
If Sophia has crossed the sea."

   Am    Em
"I own I made a bride of your daughter,
     Am   D Am  G
She's neither the better nor worse for me;
  C  Dm   Em
She came to me with a horse and saddle,
   Am    Em   Am
She may go home in a coach and three."

   Am     Em
Lord Bateman prepared another marriage
    Am   D Am  G
With both their hearts so full of glee;
   C  Dm   Em
"I'll range no more in foreign countries,
   Am    Em   Am
Now since Sophia has crossed the sea."

# The Cutty Wren

"What strikes most people about English folksongs . . . is their deep melancholy. Their style of tune comes from the Church modes of the Middle Ages and it often seems to have stamped them unmistakeably with the bitter sadness of the time of the Black Death and the baronial oppression of the 14th century. . . . The spread of a disease which, at its height, wiped out one in two people in London . . . put the finishing touch to the peasant revolt movement in 1381. The outbreak of lawlessness . . . filled the green woods with outlaws and rebels. It was about that time that the people began singing a song called 'The Cutty Wren.' . . . In countless legends the wren features as a tyrant. . . . In the song of 'The Cutty Wren' it would seem that the tyrant wren had become a symbol for baronial property, preparations for whose seizure and redistribution to the poor was such a formidable task. . . ." (A. L. Lloyd, *The Singing Englishman*)

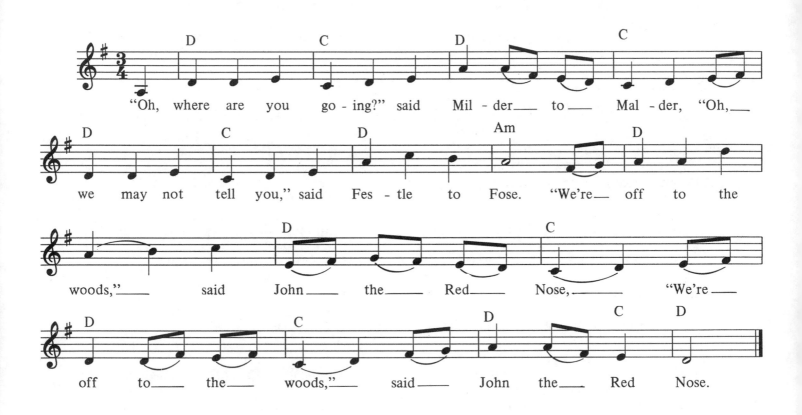

"Oh, where are you go-ing?" said Mil-der to Mal-der, "Oh, we may not tell you," said Fes-tle to Fose. "We're off to the woods," said John the Red Nose, "We're off to the woods," said John the Red Nose.

     D        C          D    C
"What will you do there?" said Milder to Malder,
     D        C          D   Am
"Oh, we may not tell you," said Festle to Fose.
        D       Am        D      C
"We'll shoot the Cutty Wren," said John the Red Nose.
        D       C       D   C D
"We'll shoot the Cutty Wren," said John the Red Nose.

     D        C          D    C
"That will not do," said Milder to Malder,
     D        C          D   Am
"Oh, what will do then?" said Festle to Fose.
        D       Am        D      C
"Big guns and big cannons," said John the Red Nose.
        D       C       D   C D
"Big guns and big cannons," said John the Red Nose.

     D        C          D    C
"How will you shoot her?" said Milder to Malder,
     D        C          D   Am
"Oh, we may not tell you," said Festle to Fose.
        D       Am        D      C
"With bows and with arrows," said John the Red Nose.
        D       C       D   C D
"With bows and with arrows," said John the Red Nose.

     D        C          D    C
"How will you bring her home?" said Milder to Malder,
     D        C          D   Am
"Oh, we may not tell you," said Festle to Fose.
        D       Am        D      C
"On four strong men's shoulders," said John the Red Nose.
        D       C       D   C D
"On four strong men's shoulders," said John the Red Nose.

  D    C    D    C
"That will not do," said Milder to Malder,
  D    C    D  Am
"Oh, what will do then?" said Festle to Fose.
  D   Am    D    C
"Big carts and big wagons," said John the Red Nose.
  D    C    D   C D
"Big carts and big wagons," said John the Red Nose.

  D    C    D    C
"How will you cut her up?" said Milder to Malder,
  D    C    D  Am
"Oh, we may not tell you," said Festle to Fose.
  D   Am    D    C
"With knives and with forks," said John the Red Nose.
  D    C    D   C D
"With knives and with forks," said John the Red Nose.

  D    C    D    C
"That will not do," said Milder to Malder,
  D    C    D  Am
"Oh, what will do then?" said Festle to Fose.
  D   Am    D    C
"Big hatchets and cleavers," said John the Red Nose.
  D    C    D   C D
"Big hatchets and cleavers," said John the Red Nose.

  D    C    D    C
"Who'll get the spare ribs?" said Milder to Malder,
  D    C    D  Am
"Oh, we may not tell you," said Festle to Fose.
  D   Am    D    C
"We'll give it all to the poor," said John the Red Nose.
  D    C    D   C D
"We'll give it all to the poor," said John the Red Nose.

# The Maid Freed from the Gallows

"Slack your rope, hangs-a-man, O slack it for a-while; I think I see my fa-ther com-ing, Rid-ing man-y a mile." "O fa-ther, have you brought me gold? Or have you paid my fee? Or have you come to see me hang-ing On the gal-lows tree?" "I have not brought you gold; I have not paid your fee But I have come to see you hang ing On the gal-lows tree."

*And so on for "brother," "sister," "aunt," "uncle", etc. until "true love."*

      G        F♯m
"Yes, I have brought you gold;
      G        F♯m
Yes, I have paid your fee;
      G   A   F♯7
Nor have I come to see you hanging
      G       D
On the gallows-tree."

# The Card Song

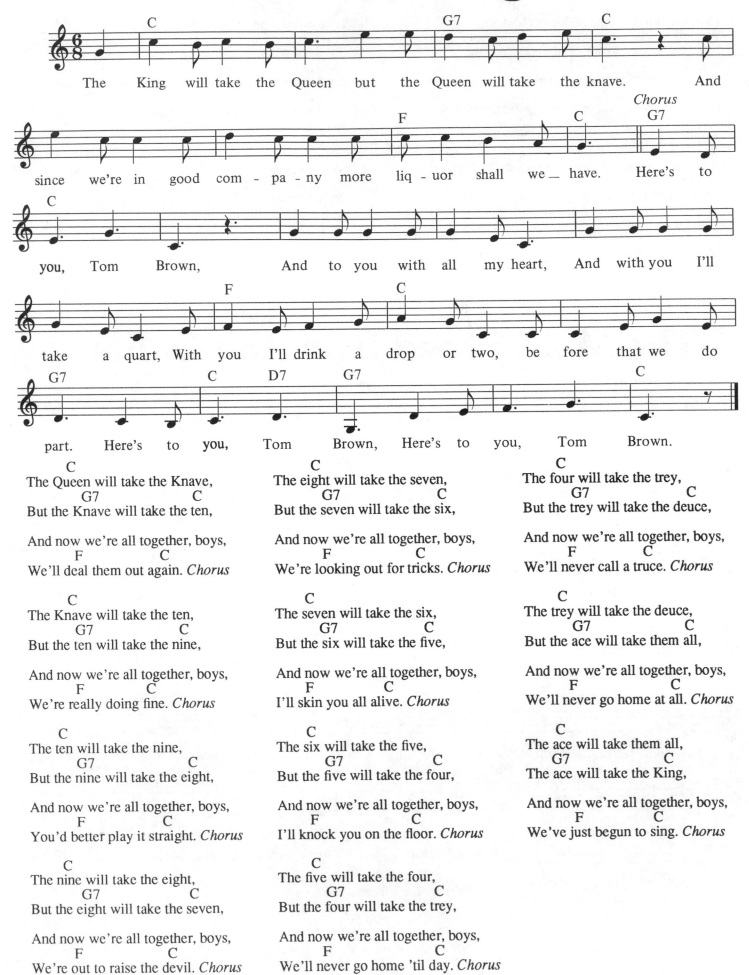

The King will take the Queen but the Queen will take the knave. And since we're in good com-pa-ny more liq-uor shall we — have. *Chorus* Here's to you, Tom Brown, And to you with all my heart, And with you I'll take a quart, With you I'll drink a drop or two, be fore that we do part. Here's to **you,** Tom Brown, Here's to you, Tom Brown.

C
The Queen will take the Knave,
G7          C
But the Knave will take the ten,

And now we're all together, boys,
F          C
We'll deal them out again. *Chorus*

C
The Knave will take the ten,
G7          C
But the ten will take the nine,

And now we're all together, boys,
F          C
We're really doing fine. *Chorus*

C
The ten will take the nine,
G7          C
But the nine will take the eight,

And now we're all together, boys,
F          C
You'd better play it straight. *Chorus*

C
The nine will take the eight,
G7          C
But the eight will take the seven,

And now we're all together, boys,
F          C
We're out to raise the devil. *Chorus*

C
The eight will take the seven,
G7          C
But the seven will take the six,

And now we're all together, boys,
F          C
We're looking out for tricks. *Chorus*

C
The seven will take the six,
G7          C
But the six will take the five,

And now we're all together, boys,
F          C
I'll skin you all alive. *Chorus*

C
The six will take the five,
G7          C
But the five will take the four,

And now we're all together, boys,
F          C
I'll knock you on the floor. *Chorus*

C
The five will take the four,
G7          C
But the four will take the trey,

And now we're all together, boys,
F          C
We'll never go home 'til day. *Chorus*

C
The four will take the trey,
G7          C
But the trey will take the deuce,

And now we're all together, boys,
F          C
We'll never call a truce. *Chorus*

C
The trey will take the deuce,
G7          C
But the ace will take them all,

And now we're all together, boys,
F          C
We'll never go home at all. *Chorus*

C
The ace will take them all,
G7          C
The ace will take the King,

And now we're all together, boys,
F          C
We've just begun to sing. *Chorus*

28

# Two Maids Went A-Milking One Day

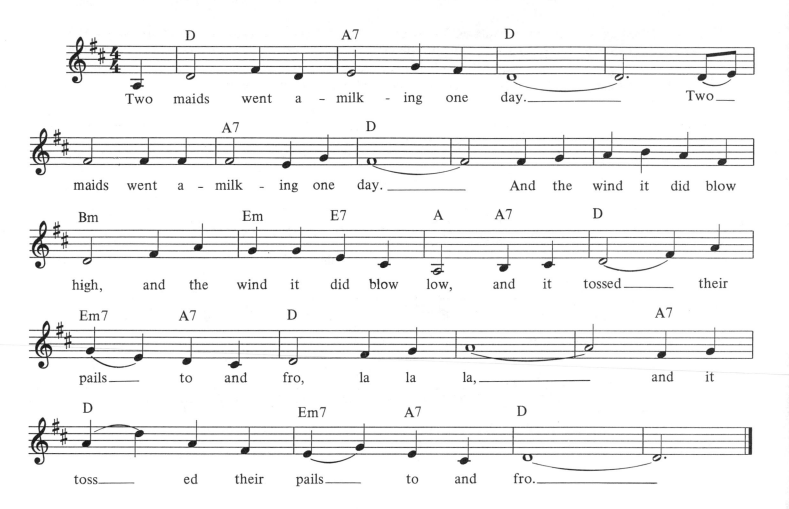

Two maids went a - milk - ing one day. _____ Two ___

maids went a - milk - ing one day. _____ And the wind it did blow

high, and the wind it did blow low, and it tossed _____ their

pails ___ to and fro, la la la, _____ and it

toss ___ ed their pails ___ to and fro. _____

 

D        A7       D
They met with a man they did know.
               A7     D
They met with a man they did know.
                        Bm
And they said, "Have you the will?"
        Em     E7     A
And they said, "Have you the skill
 A7    D    Em7 A7 D
For to catch us a small bird or two..."

            D      A7      D
"Here's a health to the blackbirds in the bush.
          A7     D
Likewise to the merry, merry doe.
               Bm
If you'll come along with me
     Em    E7    A
Under yonder flowering tree,
A7    D      Em7 A7    D
I might catch you a small bird or two."...

               D     A7     D
So they went and they sat 'neath a tree.
                 A7     D
They went and they sat 'neath two.
                     Bm
And the birds flew 'round about,
          Em    E7    A
Pretty birds flew in and out,
 A7     D       Em7 A7    D
And he caught them by one and by two...

             D     A7       D
"Now, my boys, let us drink down the sun,
                   A7    D
My boys, let us drink down the moon.
                     Bm
Take your lady to the wood,
          Em    E7    A
If you really think you should,
A7     D      Em A7    D
You might catch her a small bird or two."...

# Villikins and His Dinah

The tune of this tragi-comic British music-hall ballad has travelled to the far corners of the English-speaking world. It accompanied Sweet Betsy from Pike County, Missouri, in her covered wagon all the way to Placerville, California. During World War II, Australian soldiers sang their words to it as "Dinkie Die." It returned to Scotland in the 1950s as "The Wee Magic Stane" (recounting the theft of the Destiny Stone).

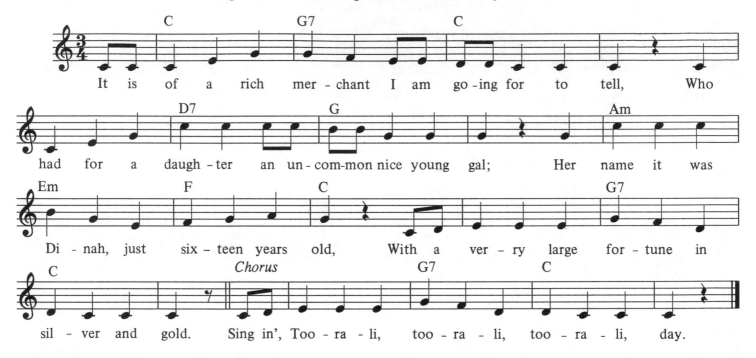

It is of a rich mer-chant I am go-ing for to tell, Who had for a daugh-ter an un-com-mon nice young gal; Her name it was Di-nah, just six-teen years old, With a ve-ry large for-tune in sil-ver and gold. Sing in', Too-ra-li, too-ra-li, too-ra-li, day.

C  G7  C
As Dinah was a-walking her garden one day,
   D7  G
Her papa he came to her, and thus he did say:
 Am  Em  F  C
"Go dress yourself, Dinah, in gorgeous array,
    G7   C
And get you a husband both gallant and gay!" *Chorus*

C  G7  C
"Oh papa, oh papa, I've not made up my mind,
   D7  G
And to marry just yet, why I don't feel inclined;
 Am  Em  F  C
To you my large fortune I'll gladly give o'er,
    G7  C
If you'll let me live single a year or two more." *Chorus*

C  G7  C
"Go, go, boldest daughter," the parent replied;
   D7  G
"If you won't consent to be this here young man's bride,
 Am  Em  F  C
I'll give your large fortune to the nearest of kin,
    G7  C
And you shan't reap the benefit of one single pin." *Chorus*

C  G7  C
As Villikins was walking the garden around,
   D7  G
He spied his dear Dinah lying dead on the ground;
 Am  Em  F  C
And a cup of cold pizen it lay by her side,
    G7  C
With a *billet-doux* stating 'twas by pizen she died. *Chorus*

C  G7  C
He kissed her cold corpus a thousand times o'er,
   D7  G
And called her his Dinah though she was no more,
 Am  Em  F
Then swallowed the pizen like a lover so brave,
    G7  C
And Villikins and his Dinah lie both in one grave. *Chorus*

     G7  C
Now all you young maidens take warning by her,
   D7  G
Never not by no means disobey your governor,
 Am  Em  F  C
And all you young fellows mind who you clap eyes on,
    G7  C
Think of Villikins and Dinah and the cup of cold pizen. *Chorus*

# The Soldier and the Sailor

Tune: Villikins and His Dinah (no chorus)

```
   C          G7         C
A soldier and a sailor were walking one day.
                   D7             G
Said the soldier to the sailor, "I've a good mind to pray
      Am       Em          F         C
For the rights of all people and the wrongs of all men.
                         G7          C
And what ever, ever I shall pray for, you must say 'Amen.'"
```

```
      C          G7            C
The first thing we'll pray for, we'll pray for some beer,
           D7        G
Glory, oh glory, it'll bring us good cheer.
    Am       Em            F            C
And if we have one pint may we also have ten—
                         G7         C
Let's have a bloody brewery. Said the sailor: Amen!
```

```
      C          G7           C
The next thing we'll pray for, we'll pray for a wench,
           D7        G
Glory, oh glory, and may she be French.
    Am       Em             F          C
And if we have one wench may we also have ten—
                     G7         C
Let's have a bloody harem. Said the sailor: Amen!
```

```
      C          G7           C
The next thing we'll pray for, we'll pray for some cash,
           D7       G
Glory, oh glory, we'll go on a bash.
    Am       Em            F          C
And if we have one pound may we also have ten—
                    G7         C
Let's have Bank of England. Said the sailor: Amen!
```

```
      C          G7          C
The next thing we'll pray for, we'll pray for a wife,
              D7        G
That we may be happy for the rest of our life.
    Am       Em           F        C
And if we have one wife may we also have ten—
                       G7       C
And another one in Tipperary. Said the sailor: Amen!
```

```
         C          G7          C
The next thing we'll pray for, we'll pray for a boat,
                    D7         G
And we don't give a damn if it sink or it float.
      Am       Em          F           C
And if we have one boat may we also have ten—
                        G7           C
Let's have the British Navy. Said the sailor: Amen!
```

```
      C          G7          C
We'll pray for the farmer who follows the plough.
                       D7           G
He makes his hard living by the sweat of his brow.
               Am       Em      F          C
We'll pray for the collier and all working men—
                            G7          C
And may all working people get together. Said the sailor: Amen!
```

```
      C          G7          C
We'll pray for the scientist in his radiation-proof room.
                       D7        G
He'll smash all your atoms and send you to the moon.
           Am          Em            F           C
He'll send you to the moon, boys, and there you'll remain—
                             G7                C
May the good Lord Almighty help you. Said the sailor: Amen!
```

```
      C          G7        C
We'll pray for the politician behind the closed doors.
                   D7        G
He'll tax your hard earnings and give you hard laws.
         Am       Em          F          C
And if you complain it's to jail you they'll send—
                         G7              C
May the rubble, dubble devil damn them. Said the sailor: Amen!
```

```
         C           G7           C
And the last thing we'll pray for, we'll pray for world peace,
                    D7          G
From Greenland to Capetown, from China to Greece.
         Am       Em            F         C
And if it lasts one year may it also last ten—
                            G7              C
May we never, never have another war. And we all say: Amen!
```

# Unfortunate Miss Bailey

Before rubber elastic was introduced, women's garters were narrow strips of knitted wool about an inch wide and nearly four feet long. They were wound around the leg below the knee three times, without tying — the ends being tucked under.

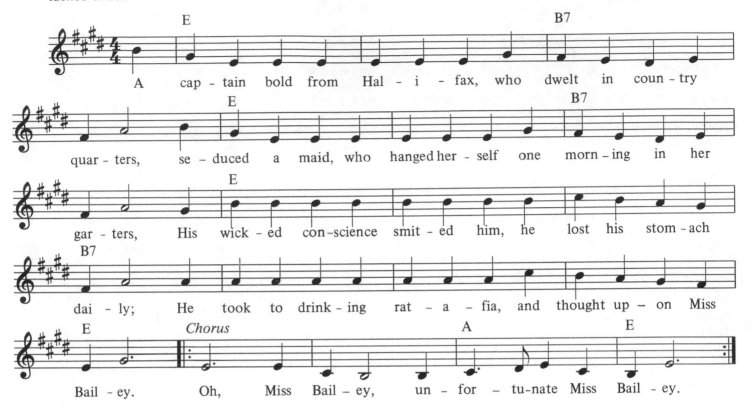

One night, betimes, he went to bed, for he had caught a fever,

Said he, "I am a handsome lad and I'm a gay deceiver."

His candle just at twelve o'clock began to burn quite palely,

A ghost stepped up to his bedside and said, "Behold! Miss Bailey!"    *Chorus*

"Avaunt, Miss Bailey," then he cried, "You can't affright me really."

"Dear Captain Smith," the ghost replied, "you've used me ungenteely."

"The coroner's 'quest was hard with me because I've acted frailly,

"And Parson Biggs won't bury me, though I'm a dead Miss Bailey."    *Chorus*

"Miss Bailey, then, since you and I accounts must once for all close,

"I've got a five-pound note in my regimental small-clothes.

"'Twill bribe the sexton for your grave." The ghost then vanished gaily,

Crying, "Bless you, wicked Captain Smith. Remember poor Miss Bailey."    *Chorus*

# Blow Away the Morning Dew

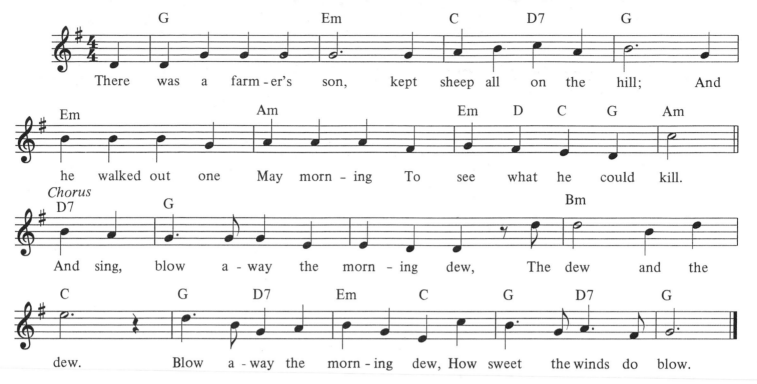

There was a farm-er's son, kept sheep all on the hill; And
he walked out one May morn-ing To see what he could kill.

*Chorus*
And sing, blow a-way the morn-ing dew, The dew and the
dew. Blow a-way the morn-ing dew, How sweet the winds do blow.

G    Em
He looked high, he looked low,
C D7 G
He cast an under look;
Em   Am
And there he saw a fair pretty maid,
Em D C G Am
Beside the watery brook. *Chorus*

G    Em
Cast over me my mantle fair
C D7 G
And pin it o'er my gown;
Em   Am
And if you will, take hold my hand,
Em D C G Am
And I will be your own. *Chorus*

G    Em
If you come down to my father's house,
C D7 G
Which is walled all around,
Em   Am
Then you shall have my maidenhead
Em D C G Am
And twenty thousand pound. *Chorus*

G    Em
He mounted on a milk-white steed,
C D7 G
And she upon another;
Em   Am
And then they rode upon the lane
Em D C G Am
Like sister and like brother. *Chorus*

G    Em
As they were riding on alone,
C D7 G
They saw some pooks of hay.
Em   Am
Oh, is this not a pretty place
Em D C G Am
For girls and boys to play? *Chorus*

G    Em
But when they came to her father's gate,
C D7 G
So nimble she popped in,
Em   Am
And said: There is a fool without,
Em D C G Am
And here's a maid within. *Chorus*

G    Em
And if you meet a lady gay
C D7 G
As you go by the hill,
Em   Am
And if you will not when you may,
Em D C G Am
You shall not when you will. *Chorus*

# Froggie Went A-Courting

Frog-gie went a court-ing and he did ride, A hum, a

hum, Frog-gie went a-court-in' and he did ride A

sword and pis-tol___ by his side, A hum, a hum,

E
He rode up to Miss Mousie's door,

A hum, a hum,
A          B7
He rode up to Miss Mousie's door.
A          B7
Where he had often been before.
E
A hum, a hum.

E
He said, "Miss Mouse, are you within?"

A hum, a hum,

He said, "Miss Mouse, are you within?"
A          B7
"Just lift the latch and please come in."
E
A hum, a hum.

E
He took Miss Mousie on his knee.

A hum, a hum,
A
He took Miss Mousie on his knee,
A              B7
And said, "Miss Mousie, will you marry me?"
E
A hum, a hum.

E
"Without my uncle Rat's consent,"

A hum, a hum,

"Without my uncle Rat's consent,
A          B7
I would not marry the president."
E
A hum, a hum.

E
Now, uncle Rat, when he came home,

A hum, a hum,

Now, uncle Rat, when he came home,
A          B7
Said, "Who's been here since I've been gone?"
E
A hum, a hum.

E
"A very fine gentleman has been here,"

A hum, a hum,

"A very fine gentleman has been here,
A          B7
Who wishes me to be his dear."
E
A hum, a hum.

```
         E
Then uncle Rat laughed and shook his sides,

   A hum, a hum,

Then uncle Rat laughed and shook his sides,
     A                    B7
 To think his niece would be a bride,
       E
   A hum, a hum.


         E
So, uncle Rat, he went to town,

   A hum, a hum,

Uncle Rat, he went to town
     A              B7
 To buy his niece a wedding gown.
         E
   A hum, a hum.


       E
Where will the wedding breakfast be?

   A hum, a hum,

Where will the wedding breakfast be?
 A                        B7
Away down yonder in the hollow tree.
         E
   A hum, a hum.


       E
What will the wedding breakfast be?

   A hum, a hum,

What will the wedding breakfast be?
A                    B7
Two green beans and a black-eyed pea.
       E
   A hum a hum.
```

```
         E
The first to come was bumblebee.

   A hum, a hum,

The first to come was the bumblebee;
     A                B7
He danced a jig with Miss Mousie.
       E
   A hum, a hum.


         E
The next to come was Mister Drake.

   A hum, a hum,

The next to come was Mister Drake,
   A                    B7
He ate up all of the wedding cake.
         E
   A hum, a hum.


         E
They all went sailing on the lake,

   A hum, a hum,

They all went sailing on the lake,
     A                          B7
And they all got swallowed by a big black snake.
       E
   A hum, a hum.


         E
So, that's the end of one, two, three,

   A hum, a hum,

That's the end of one, two, there,
   A              B7
The Rat, the Frog and Miss Mousie.
         E
   A hum, a hum.
```

```
             E
There's bread and cheese upon the shelf,

   A hum, a hum,

There's bread and cheese upon the shelf,
         A              B7
If you want any more just sing it yourself.
         E
   A hum, a hum.
```

# Greensleeves

"The earliest mention of the ballad of *Green Sleeves* in the registers of the Stationers' Company is in September 1580, when Richard Jones had licensed to him 'A new Northern Dittye of the *Lady Greene Sleeves.*'... On the 24th of August, 1581 ... Edward White had licensed 'a ballad intituled —

> Greene Sleeves is worne awaie,
> Yellow Sleeves come to decaie.
> Blacke Sleeves I hold in despite,
> But White Sleeves is my delight.'

"Shakespeare, in *The Merry Wives of Windsor*, twice makes mention of the tune:
*Falstaff.* 'Let the sky rain potatoes! let it thunder to the tune of *Green Sleeves....*' Act v, Sc. 5.
*Mrs. Ford.* 'I shall think the worse of fat men ... they do no more adhere and keep pace together, than the Hundreth Psalm to the tune of *Green Sleeves.*' Act ii, Sc. 1.

"... In ... the Society of Antiquaries are copies of 'A Warning to false Traitors, by example of fourteen; whereof six were executed in divers places neere about London, and two near Braintford, the 28th day of August, 1588; also at Tyburne were executed the 30th day six; viz., five men and one woman: to the tune of *Green Sleeves.*'..."
(William Chappell, *Old English Popular Music,* London, 1836)

| Em          D | Em          D | Em          D |
|---|---|---|

Em          D
I have been ready at your hand
Em          B7
To grant whatever you would crave;
Em          D
I have both wagered life and land,
    Em    B7    Em
Your love and good will for to have.    *Chorus*

Em          D
I bought thee kerchiefs to thy head
Em          B7
That were wrought fine and gallantly;
Em          D
I kept thee both at board and bed,
    Em    B7    Em
Which cost my purse well favoredly.    *Chorus*

Em          D
Thy smock of gold so crimson red,
Em          B7
With pearls bedecked sumptuously.
Em          D
The like no other lasses had,
    Em    B7    Em
And yet thou wouldest not love me.    *Chorus*

Em          D
Thy gown was of the grassy green,
Em          B7
Thy sleeves of satin hanging by;
Em          D
Which made thee be our harvest queen,
    Em    B7    Em
And yet thou wouldest not love me.    *Chorus*

Em          D
Thou couldst desire no earthly thing,
Em          B7
But still thou hadst it readily;
Em          D
Thy music still to play and sing,
    Em    B7    Em
And yet thou wouldest not love me.    *Chorus*

Em          D
Well, I pray to God on high
Em          B7
That thou my constancy mayst see;
Em          D
And that yet once before I die
    Em    B7    Em
Thou wilt vouchsafe to love me.    *Chorus*

*Last Verse*    Em          D
Greensleeves, now farewell, adieu!
Em          B7
God I pray to prosper thee;
Em          D
For I am still thy lover true,
    Em B7    Em
Come once again and love me.    *Chorus*

# Rue

The plant rue was much used in Medieval and later medicine as a stimulant and irritant drug. It was commonly supposed to be much used by witches. It was known as the "herb of grace," and was taken as the symbol of repentance. As to the significance of thyme: Under the heading "LABIATAE (i.e. *'lipped'*) . . . seed plants," in the 1911 edition of the *Encyclopedia Britannica* we find this suggestive description: ". . . The stames and style lie on the under lip and honey is secreted on the upper side. . . . The insect in probing the flower gets smeared with pollen on its belly and legs. . . ." In the same edition, under the heading "BALNEOTHERAPEUTICS," there is a description of the use of baths taken with hot infusions of thyme, which "have very great value . . . in some of the special troubles of women."

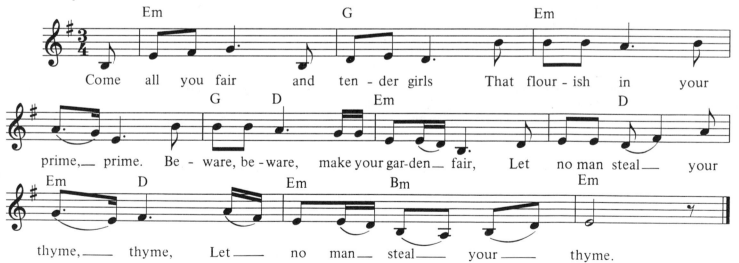

And when your thyme is past and gone
Em          G
He'll care no more for you.
  G    D       Em
And every day that your garden is waste
    D    Em D
Will spread all over with rue, rue.
Em    Bm    Em
Will spread all over with rue.

Em          G
A woman is a branched tree
Em
And man a singing wind.
  G    D       Em
And from her branches carelessly
    D    Em D
He'll take what he can find, find.
Em    Bm    Em
He'll take what he can find.

# Down, Down, Derry Down

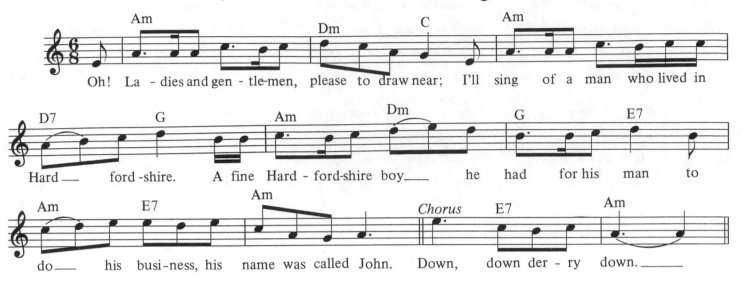

Oh! La - dies and gen - tle-men, please to draw near; I'll sing of a man who lived in Hard — ford -shire. A fine Hard - ford-shire boy___ he had for his man to do___ his busi-ness, his name was called John. Down, down der - ry down. ___

*Chorus*

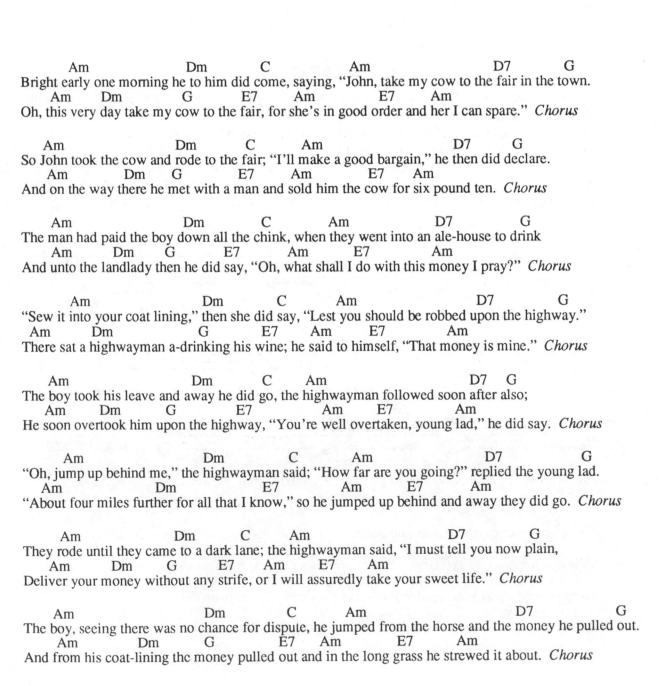

Am                Dm            C          Am                      D7        G
Bright early one morning he to him did come, saying, "John, take my cow to the fair in the town.
Am    Dm      G       E7     Am        E7    Am
Oh, this very day take my cow to the fair, for she's in good order and her I can spare." *Chorus*

Am                 Dm            C          Am                    D7      G
So John took the cow and rode to the fair; "I'll make a good bargain," he then did declare.
Am        Dm     G        E7     Am       E7    Am
And on the way there he met with a man and sold him the cow for six pound ten. *Chorus*

Am                       Dm            C          Am            D7                G
The man had paid the boy down all the chink, when they went into an ale-house to drink
Am     Dm     G        E7     Am       E7         Am
And unto the landlady then he did say, "Oh, what shall I do with this money I pray?" *Chorus*

Am                    Dm          C          Am               D7              G
"Sew it into your coat lining," then she did say, "Lest you should be robbed upon the highway."
Am      Dm       G       E7      Am      E7        Am
There sat a highwayman a-drinking his wine; he said to himself, "That money is mine." *Chorus*

Am                   Dm          C          Am                D7       G
The boy took his leave and away he did go, the highwayman followed soon after also;
Am      Dm      G         E7        Am       E7        Am
He soon overtook him upon the highway, "You're well overtaken, young lad," he did say. *Chorus*

Am                   Dm            C           Am                       D7              G
"Oh, jump up behind me," the highwayman said; "How far are you going?" replied the young lad.
Am          Dm            E7       Am       E7        Am
"About four miles further for all that I know," so he jumped up behind and away they did go. *Chorus*

Am                   Dm            C          Am               D7             G
They rode until they came to a dark lane; the highwayman said, "I must tell you now plain,
Am      Dm       G        E7     Am        E7      Am
Deliver your money without any strife, or I will assuredly take your sweet life." *Chorus*

Am                    Dm          C          Am                       D7                G
The boy, seeing there was no chance for dispute, he jumped from the horse and the money he pulled out.
Am        Dm      G        E7      Am      E7        Am
And from his coat-lining the money pulled out and in the long grass he strewed it about. *Chorus*

```
         Am                      Dm              C         Am              D7         G
The highwayman immediately jumped from his horse, but little he judged it was for his loss,
         Am       Dm      G      E7        Am         E7           Am
For while he was putting it into his purse, the boy took his leave and rode off with the horse. *Chorus*


         Am                      Dm              C         Am                   D7         G
The highwayman hollooed and bade him to stay, the boy never minded but still rode away,
        Am     Dm          G           E7        Am    E7            Am
And unto his master's house he did bring horse, saddle and bridle and many fine thing. *Chorus*


         Am                      Dm         C         Am                        D7        G
On searching the saddle-bags, as we are told, there were ten thousand pounds in silver and gold,
       Am        Dm         G        E7     Am           E7              Am
Beside two bright pistols—the boy said, "I trow, I think, my dear master, I've sold well your cow!" *Chorus*


         Am                  Dm       C         Am                   D7        G
His master smiled when him had told, saying, "As for a boy you've been very bold,
      Am          Dm           G        E7       Am      E7        Am
As for the highwayman, he's lost all his store, let him go a-robbing until he gets more." *Chorus*
```

# Byker Hill

I recorded this Tyneside miners' song from the singing of British physicist John Hasted on June 16, 1958.

Oh, if I had an-oth-er pen-ny, Then I'd have an-oth-er jill,

I'd make the pip-er play, "The Bon-nie Lass of By-ker Hill."

```
                                              C
                                    The pitman and the keelman trim,
                                       G7                C
                                    They drink bumbo made of gin,
                                       F
                                    Then to dance they all begin,
                                       C              Am
                                    To the tune of "Elsie Marley".   Chorus
```

```
                      C                                C
Chorus:    Byker Hill and Walker Shore,        When first I went down to the dirt,
                      G7         C                    G7                C
           Collier lads forevermore;           I had no cowl and no pit-shirt,
                      F                                F
           Byker Hill and Walker Shore,        Now I've gotten two or three,
                      C          Am                    C            Am
           Collier lads forevermore.           Walker Pit's done well for me.   Chorus
```

```
                                    C
                                    Now Geordie Johnson he had a pig,
                                       G7                          C
                                    He hit it with a shovel and it danced a jig,
                                       F
                                    All the way to Duncan's rig,
                                       C              Am
                                    To the tune of "Elsie Marley".   Chorus
```

39

# John Peel

Words by John W. Graves
Music: Bonnie Annie

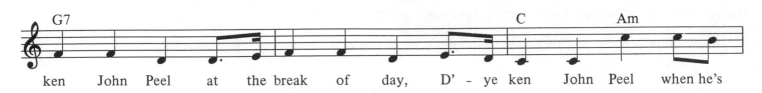

D' - ye ken John Peel with his coat so gay? D'ye

ken John Peel at the break of day, D' - ye ken John Peel when he's

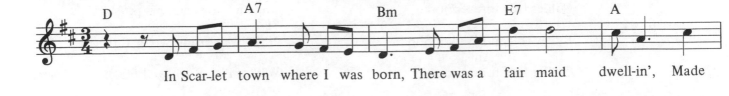

far, far a - way, With his hounds and his horn in the morn — ing?

             C
'Twas the sound of his horn brought me from my bed,
    G7
And the cry of his hounds which he oftimes led,
    C          Am          F    C
For Peel's "View Halloo!" would awaken the dead,
A7  Dm      G7        C
Or the fox from his lair in the morning.

        C
Yes, I ken John Peel and Ruby too!
 G7
Ranter and Ringwood, Bellman and True.
     C      Am      F    C
From a find to a check, from a check to a view,
  A7  Dm     G7        C
With a view to a death in the morning.

             C
D'ye ken John Peel with his coat so gay?
          G7
He lived at Troutbeck once on a day,
            C   Am  F  C
Now he has gone far, far away,
  A7     Dm          G7         C
We shall ne'er hear his voice in the morning.

# Barbara Allen

"Few ballads have had a more lasting popularity than 'Cruel Barbara Allen.'... Early forms of it are found on black letter broadsides, and a mention is made by Pepys in his diary under January 2nd, 1665...." (William Chappell, *Old English Popular Music,* London, 1836)

In Scar-let town where I was born, There was a fair maid dwell-in', Made

ev -'ry youth cry—— "Well a - day," Her name was Bar – b'ry El - len.

```
D           A7        Bm
 'Twas in the merry month of May,
            E7        A
When green buds, they were swellin',
       G              D
Sweet William on his death-bed lay.
     A7           D
For the love of Barbara Allen.


D           A7        Bm
 He sent his servant to the town,
          E7        A
Where Barb'ry was a-dwellin',
   G              D
"My master's sick and bids you come,
     A7           D
If your name be Barbara Allen."


D           A7        Bm
 So slowly, slowly got she up,
         E7        A
And slowly she came nigh him.
  G              D
And all she said when she got there,
       A7           D
"Young man, I think you're dyin'."


D           A7        Bm
 "Oh yes, I'm sick and very sick,
        E7        A
For death is in me dwellin'.
  G              D
No better can I ever be,
   A7           D
If I can't have Barbara Allen."


D           A7              Bm
 Then lightly tripped she down the stairs,
         E7        A
He trembled like an aspen.
     G              D
"'Tis vain, 'tis vain, my dear young man,
        A7    D
To pine for Barbara Allen."
```

```
D           A7        Bm
 He turned his pale face to the wall,
          E7        A
For death was in him dwellin'.
   G              D
"Adieu, adieu, my friends all 'round,
     A7           D
Be kind to Barbara Allen."


D           A7              Bm
 As she went down the long piney walk,
          E7        A
The birds, they kept a-singin'.
     G              D
They sang so clear, they seemed to say,
        A7           D
"Hard-hearted Barbara Allen."


D           A7                  Bm
 She looked to the east, she looked to the west,
          E7        A
She spied his corpse a-comin'.
   G              D
"Lay down, lay down that deathly frame,
     A7           D
That I may look upon him."


D            A7            Bm
 "Farewell," she said, "ye virgins, all,
          E7        A
And shun the fault I fell in.
     G              D
Henceforth take warning by the fall
     A7           D
Of cruel Barbara Allen."


D           A7              Bm
 They buried her in the old church yard,
             E7        A
And he was buried nigh her.
     G              D
On William's grave grew a red, red rose.
     A7              D
On Barb'ra's grew a brier.
```

```
        D              A7            Bm
 They grew to the top of the old church wall,
            E7        A
'Til they could grow no higher,
        G              D
And there they tied a true lover's knot,
        A7              D
The red rose 'round the brier.
```

# Lady Isabel and the Elf Knight

There was a lord in Lon — don town, He court-ed a la — dy gay, ____ And all that he court-ed this la — dy for Was to take her sweet life a — way.

"Come give to me of your father's gold,
Likewise your mother's fee,
And two of the best horses in your father's stable,
For there stand thirty and three."

She mounted on her milk-white steed,
And he the fast travelling grey,
They rode till he came to the seashore side,
Three hours before it was day.

"Alight, alight, my pretty Polly,
Alight, alight," said he,
"For six pretty maids I have drownded here,
And you the seventh shall be."

"Now take off your silken dress,
Likewise your golden stay,
For I think your clothing too rich and too gay
To rot all in the salt sea."

"Yes, I'll take off my silken dress,
Likewise my golden stay,
But before I do, so, you false young man,
You must face yon willow tree."

Then he turned his back around,
And faced yon willow tree,
She caught him around the middle so small,
And throwed him into the sea.

And as he rose and as he sank,
And as he rose, said he,
"O give me your hand, my pretty Polly,
My bride forever you'll be."

"Lie there, lie there, you false young man,
Lie there instead of me,
For six pretty maids you've drownded here,
And the seventh one has drownded thee."

She lighted on her milk-white steed,
And led the fast travelling grey,
And rode till she came to her to her father's outside,
One hour before it was day.

The parrot in the garret so high,
And unto pretty Polly did say,
"What's the matter, my pretty Polly,
You're driving before it is day?"

"No tales, no tales, my pretty Polly,
No tales, no tales," said she,
"Your cage will be made of the glittering gold,
Likewise of ivory."

"No tales, no tales, my pretty Polly,
No tales, no tales," said she,
"Your cage will be made of the glittering gold,
And hung on yon willow tree."

# The Three Ravens

This song first appeared in print in *Melismata* (1611). Sir Walter Scott included the Scottish version, under the title "The Twa Corbies," in his *Minstrelsy of the Scottish Borders* (1827).

Em          Am      B(7)    Em      C
There were three rav - ens sat on a tree, Down, a down, hey

Em      B(7)      Em          Am
down a down. They were as black as black might be with a

G      Bm         Em         F♯m
down._____ The one of them said to his mate,

*Chorus*

Em         B(7)        Em  Am    B(7)    E
"Where shall— we our break-fast take?" With a down. der-ry, der-ry, der-ry down down.

Em          Am B7
Down in yonder green field,
Em    C     Em     B7
Down a down, hey down a down,
    Em         Am
There lies a knight slain under his shield,
     G Bm
  With a down.
    Em         F♯m
His hounds they lie down at his feet,
    Em        B7
So well do they their master keep. *Chorus*

Em          Am B7
She lifted up his bloody head,
Em    C     Em     B7
Down a down, hey down a down,
    Em         Am
And kissed his wounds that were so red,
     G Bm
  With a down.
    Em         F♯m
She got him up upon her back,
    Em        B7
And carried him to earthen lake. *Chorus*

Em          Am B7
His hawks they fly so eagerly,
Em    C     Em     B7
Down a down, hey down a down,
    Em         Am
No other fowl dare come him nigh,
     G Bm
  With a down.
Em          F♯m
Down there comes a fallow doe,
    Em        B7
As heavy with young as she might go. *Chorus*

Em          Am     B7
She buried him before the prime,
Em    C     Em     B7
Down a down, hey down a down,
    Em         Am
She was dead herself 'ere even-song time,
     G Bm
  With a down.
Em          F♯m
God send every gentleman
    Em        B7
Such hawks, such hounds and such leman. *Chorus*

43

# The Wraggle-Taggle Gypsies

There— were three gyp-sies a – come to my door And down-stairs ran this a la – dy – o.

One sang high and the oth-er sang low, And the oth-er sang of bon–ny, bon–ny Bis – cay, o!

|  |  |  |
|---|---|---|
| Dm      A7      Dm | | |

        Dm           A7         Dm
Then she pulled off her silk-finished gown,
      B♭    C7     F
And put on hose of leather - o.
        Am          Dm F    Gm
The ragged, ragged rags about our door,
          Dm         A7       Dm
And she's gone with the wraggle-taggle gypsies-o!

        Dm           A7         Dm
It was late last night when my lord came home,
      B♭    C7     F
Inquiring for his a-lady-o.
         Am   Dm F    Gm
The servants said on every hand:
        Dm        A7       Dm
She's gone with the wraggle-taggle gypsies-o.

        Dm          A7       Dm
O, saddle to me my milk-white steed,
      B♭     C7     F
And go fetch me my pony - o!
        Am        Dm    Gm
That I may ride and seek my bride,
        Dm        A7        Dm
Who is gone with the wraggle-taggle gypsies-o.

    Dm          A7    Dm
O, he rode high and he rode low,
      B♭        C7      F
He rode through woods and copses - o,
    Am Dm    F      Gm
Until came to a wide open field,
     Dm   A7    Dm
A-there he espied his a-lady-o.

         Dm          A7        Dm
What makes you leave your house and land?
      B♭     C7        F
What makes you leave your money - o?
         Am        Dm      F         Gm
What makes you leave your new-wedded lord
         Dm         A7         Dm
To go with the wraggle-taggle gypsies-o?

         Dm          A7        Dm
What care I for my house and land?
      B♭ C7       F
What care I for my money - o?
        Am Dm     F         Gm
What care I for my new-wedded lord?
        Dm         A7         Dm
I'm off with the wraggle-taggle gypsies-o!

         Dm          A7         Dm
Last night you slept on a goose-feather bed,
      B♭       C7      F
With the sheet turned down so bravely - o!
        Am        Dm      F        Gm
Tonight you'll sleep in a cold, open field,
        Dm         A7         Dm
Along with the wraggle-taggle gypsies-o!

         Dm       A7         Dm
What care I for a goose-feather bed,
      B♭        C7      F
With the sheet turned down so bravely - o!
        Am        Dm      F         Gm
For tonight I shall sleep in a cold, open field,
        Dm       A7         Dm
Along with the wraggle-taggle gypsies-o!

# Lord Lovel

Francis J. Child (1825–1896), whose monumental collection, *The English and Scottish Popular Ballads*, is the authoritative treasury of its subject, cited the earliest appearance of the text of "Lord Lovel" in an 1846 London broadside. However, a still earlier example of the song was printed in *The New England Songster*, Portsmouth, New Hampshire, in 1832.

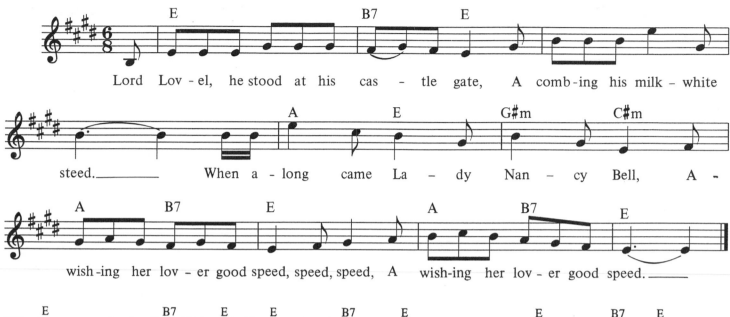

Lord Lov-el, he stood at his cas-tle gate, A comb-ing his milk-white steed._____ When a-long came La-dy Nan-cy Bell, A-wish-ing her lov-er good speed, speed, speed, A wish-ing her lov-er good speed._____

| E | B7 | E |
|---|---|---|
"Oh, where are you going, Lord Lovel?" she said.

"Oh, where are you going?" said she.
    A   E   G#m C#m
"I'm going, my dear Lady Nancy Bell,
    A   B7   E
Strange countries for to see, see, see,
    A   B7   E
Strange countries for to see."

| E | B7 | E |
|---|---|---|
He mounted on his milk-white steed,

And he rode to London Town,
    A   E   G#m C#m
And there he heard St. Varney's bell,
    A   B7   E
And the people all mourning around, 'round, 'round.
    A   B7   E
And the people all mourning around.

| E | B7 | E |
|---|---|---|
Lady Nancy died as it might be today,

Lord Lovel, he died tomorrow.
    A   E  G#m  C#m
Lady Nancy, she died of pure, pure grief,
    A   B7   E
Lord Lovel, he died of sorrow, row, row,
    A   B7   E
Lord Lovel, he died of sorrow.

| E | B7 | E |
|---|---|---|
"When will you be back, Lord Lovel?" she said.

"When will you be back?" said she.
    A   E   G#m C#m
"In a year or two, or three at most,
    A   B7   E
I'll return to my Lady Nancy, cy, cy,
    A   B7   E
I'll return to my Lady Nancy."

| E | B7 | E |
|---|---|---|
"Is anyone dead?" Lord Lovel, he said.

"Is anyone dead?" said he.
    A   E   G#m C#m
"A lady is dead," the people all said,
    A   B7   E
"And they call her Lady Nancy, cy, cy,
    A   B7   E
And they call her Lady Nancy."

| E | B7 | E |
|---|---|---|
Lady Nancy was laid in St. Clement's churchyard,

Lord Lovel was laid in the choir.
    A   E   G#m C#m
And out of her bosom there grew a red rose,
    A   B7   E
And out of his backbone a brier, brier, brier,
    A   B7   E
And out of his backbone a brier.

| E | B7 | E |
|---|---|---|
He'd not been gone twelve months and a day,

Strange countries for to see,
    A   E   G#m C#m
When languishing thoughts came to his mind,
    A   B7   E
"Lady Nancy Bell must see, see, see,
    A   B7   E
Lady Nancy Bell I must see."

| E | B7 | E |
|---|---|---|
He ordered the grave to be opened forthwith,

The shroud to be folded down.
    A   E   G#m C#m
And then he kissed her clay cold lips,
    A   B7   E
'Til the tears came trickling down, down, down,
    A   B7   E
'Til the tears came trickling down.

| E | B7 | E |
|---|---|---|
So then they entwined the true lovers' way,

For all the true lovers to admire.
    A   E   G#m C#m
And ever since then the roses are red,
    A   B7   E
And sharp, indeed, is the brier, brier, brier,
    A   B7   E
And sharp, indeed, is the brier.

# The Bailiff's Daughter of Islington

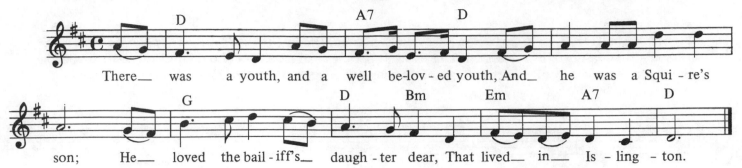

There— was a youth, and a well be-lov-ed youth, And— he was a Squi-re's son; He— loved the bail-iff's— daugh-ter dear, That lived— in— Is-ling-ton.

D       A7     D
Yet she was coy and would not believe

That he did love her so.
G        D     Bm
No nor at any time would she
Em    A7    D
Any countenance to him show.

D       A7 D
But when his friends did understand

His fond and foolish mind,
G        D     Bm
They sent him up to fair London Town
Em    A7    D
As apprentice for to bind.

D       A7 D
Then all the maids of Islington

Went forth to sport and play.
G        D     Bm
All but the bailiff's daughter dear,
Em    A7    D
She secretly stole away.

D       A7     D
She pulled off her gown of green

And put on ragged attire,
G        D     Bm
And to fair London she would go,
Em    A7    D
Her true love to enquire.

D       A7     G
As she went down the king's highway,

The weather being hot and dry,
G        D     Bm
She sat her down upon a green bank,
Em    A7    D
And her true love came riding by.

D       A7     D
She started up with a color so red,

Catching hold of his bridle rein:
G        D     Bm
"One penny, one penny, kind sir," she said,
Em    A7    D
"Will ease me of much pain."

D       A7     D
"Before I give you one penny, sweetheart,

Pray tell me where you were born."
G        D     Bm
"At Islington, kind sir," she said,
Em    A7    D
"Where I've had many a scorn."

D       A7     D
"I prithee, sweetheart, tell to me,

O tell me whether you know
G        D     Bm
The bailiff's daughter of Islington."
Em    A7    D
"She's dead, sir, long ago."

D       A7     D
"If she be dead, then take my horse,

My saddle and bridle also;
G        D     Bm
For I will into some far country,
Em    A7    D
Where no man shall me know."

D       A7     D
"O stay, o stay, thou goodly youth,

She standeth by thy side.
G        D     Bm
She is here alive, she is not dead,
Em    A7    D
And ready to be your bride."

D       A7     D
"O farewell grief and welcome joy,

Ten thousand times therefore,
G        D     Bm
For now I have found my own true love,
Em    A7    D
Whom I thought I should never see more."

# My Mother Chose My Husband

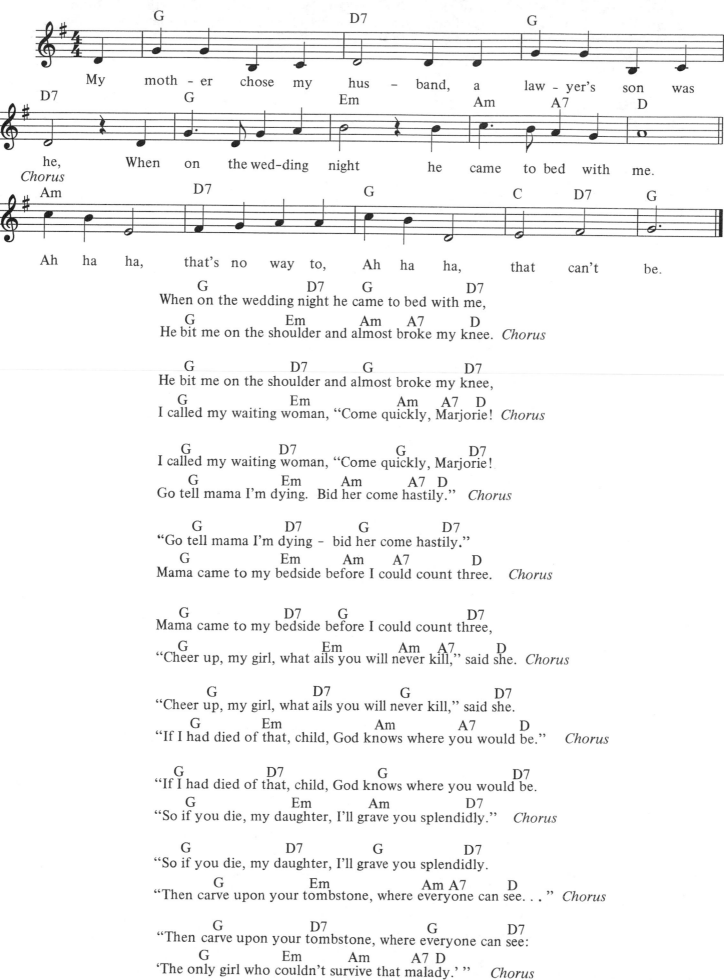

My moth-er chose my hus-band, a law-yer's son was he, When on the wed-ding night he came to bed with me.

*Chorus*

Ah ha ha, that's no way to, Ah ha ha, that can't be.

                 G           D7   G        D7
When on the wedding night he came to bed with me,
                 G       Em      Am  A7     D
He bit me on the shoulder and almost broke my knee. *Chorus*

                 G           D7   G        D7
He bit me on the shoulder and almost broke my knee,
                 G       Em         Am  A7 D
I called my waiting woman, "Come quickly, Marjorie! *Chorus*

                 G           D7       G        D7
I called my waiting woman, "Come quickly, Marjorie!
           G       Em     Am      A7 D
Go tell mama I'm dying. Bid her come hastily." *Chorus*

                 G           D7       G        D7
"Go tell mama I'm dying - bid her come hastily."
           G       Em     Am   A7      D
Mama came to my bedside before I could count three. *Chorus*

                 G           D7   G          D7
Mama came to my bedside before I could count three,
              G          Em     will you never Am A7    D
"Cheer up, my girl, what ails you will never kill," said she. *Chorus*

                 G           D7       G        D7
"Cheer up, my girl, what ails you will never kill," said she.
            G       Em     Am      A7      D
"If I had died of that, child, God knows where you would be." *Chorus*

                 G          D7       G         D7
"If I had died of that, child, God knows where you would be.
             G       Em     Am      D
"So if you die, my daughter, I'll grave you splendidly." *Chorus*

                 G          D7       G        D7
"So if you die, my daughter, I'll grave you splendidly.
           G      Em          Am A7      D
"Then carve upon your tombstone, where everyone can see. . ." *Chorus*

                 G           D7       G        D7
"Then carve upon your tombstone, where everyone can see:
           G      Em     Am      A7 D
'The only girl who couldn't survive that malady.' " *Chorus*

# Queen Jane

Jane Seymour was the third wife of Henry VIII. On October 12, 1537, she gave birth to the future Edward VI. The birth was a natural one and not, as the ballad describes, by Caesarian section. Her death twelve days later was due to a poorly treated infection.

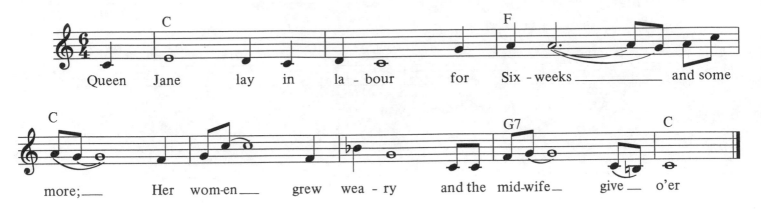

O, women, kind women, as I know you to be,
Pray cut my side open and save my baby.

O, no, said the women, that never might be!
We'll send for King Henry in the hour of your need.

King Henry was sent for by horseback and speed,
King Henry he come there in the hour of her need,

King Henry he come in and stood by her bed.
What ails my pretty flower, her eyes look so red.

O, Henry, kind Henry, pray listen to me,
Pray cut my side open and save my baby.

O, no, said King Henry, that never might be!
I'd lose my pretty flower to save my baby.

Queen Jane she turned over and fell in a swound,
They cut her side open, her baby was found.

How black was the mourning, how yellow her bed;
How white the bright shroud in which Queen Jane was laid.

Six followed after, six bore her along.
King Henry come after, his head hanging down.

King Henry he wept 'til his hands were wrung sore,
Says, the flower of England is blooming no more.

That baby was christened the very next day;
His mother's poor body lay mouldering away.

48

# The Darby Ram

A totemistic song, akin to "The Cutty Wren."

As I was going to Dar - by up - on a mar - ket

day,_____ I saw the big - gest ram, sir, That ev - er was fed on hay;_____ _____ that ev - er was fed on hay._____

         A  
The ram was fat behind, sir,  
      E7   A  
The ram was fat before.  
  Bm          E  
He measured ten yards round, sir,  
  D   E7     A  
I think it was no more. (2)

         A  
And he who knocked this ram down  
        E7   A  
Was drowned in the blood,  
  Bm         E  
And he who held the dish, sir,  
    D   E7    A  
Was carried away by the flood. (2)

         A  
The wool grew on his back, sir,  
      E7   A  
It reached to the sky.  
  Bm         E  
And there the eagles built their nests,  
  D   E7     A  
I heard the young ones cry. (2)

         A  
And all the boys in Darby, sir,  
      E7    A  
Came begging for his eyes,  
  Bm        E  
To kick about the street, sir,  
  D   E7    A  
As any good football flies. (2)

         A  
The wool grew on his belly, sir,  
      E7   A  
It reached to the ground.  
  Bm        E  
It was sold in Darby Town, sir,  
  D   E7    A  
For forty thousand pound. (2)

         A  
The wool upon his tail, sir,  
          E7  A  
Filled more than fifty bags.  
  Bm        E  
You'd better keep away, sir,  
    D   E7    A  
When that tail shakes and wags. (2)

         A  
The horns upon his head, sir,  
       E7     A  
As high as a man could reach,  
  Bm        E  
And there they built a pulpit, sir,  
    D   E7   A  
The Quakers for to preach. (2)

         A  
And one of this ram's teeth, sir,  
      E7   A  
Was hollow as a horn;  
  Bm        E  
And when they took its measure, sir,  
    D   E7   A  
It held a bushel of corn. (2)

         A  
The mutton that the ram made  
            E7    A  
Gave the whole Army meat,  
  Bm        E  
And what was left, I'm told, sir,  
    D   E7   A  
Was served out to the fleet. (2)

         A  
The man who owned this ram, sir,  
           E7   A  
Was considered mighty rich,  
    Bm        E  
But the man who told this story, sir,  
    D   E7   A  
Was a lyin' son-of-a-bitch. (2)

# The Vicar of Bray

Bray is a small village in Berkshire on the banks of the Thames. The song is historically significant enough to have warranted the following mention in the 1911 edition of the *Encyclopedia Britannica:* "A well-known ballad, 'The Vicar of Bray,' tells how a vicar held his position by easy conversions of faith according to necessity, from the days of Charles II until the accession of George I of 'the illustrious house of Hanover' (1714). One Francis Carswell, who is buried in the church, was vicar for forty-two years, approximately during this period, dying in 1709; but the legend is earlier, and the name of the vicar who gave rise to it is not certainly known. That of Simon Aleyn, who held the office from *c.* 1540 to 1588, is generally accepted, as, in the reigns of Henry VIII, Edward VI, Mary and Elizabeth, he is said to have been successively Papist, Protestant, Papist and Protestant. . . . Tradition ascribes the song to a soldier in Colonel Fuller's troop of dragoons in the reign of George I."

In good King Charles es gold-en time, When loy-al-ty no harm meant. A
zeal-ous high church-man was I, And so I gained pre-fer-ment. To
teach my flock I nev-er missed, Kings are by God ap-point-ed, And
damned are those who dare re-sist, Or touch the Lord's a-noint-ed. And
this is law, that I'll main-tain, Un-til my dy-ing day, sir, That
what so-ev-er king may reign, Still I'll be the Vic-ar of Bray, sir!

|  |  |  |
|---|---|---|
| C       G7    C | | C       G7  C |

              C              G7       C
When Royal James possessed the crown,
      F    G7 C
And popery came in fashion,
                 G7     C
The Penal Laws I hooted down,
          F  G7 C
And read the Declaration.
             Am     G    Am   Em
The Church of Rome I found did fit
             Am     G  D7 G
Full well my constitution.
            C          G7 C
And I had been a Jesuit,
          F G7 C
But for the Revolution.   *Chorus*

              C              G7  C
When William was our King declared,
             F     G7 C
To ease the nation's grievance,
                 G7     C
With this new wind about I steered
                 F   G7 C
And swore to him allegiance.
            Am G    Am  Em
Old principles I did revoke,
             Am     G   D7 G
Set conscience at a distance,
           C           G7     C
Passive obedience was a joke,
                 F   G7 C
A jest was non-resistance.  *Chorus*

```
        C              G7        C
When Royal Anne became our queen,
                 F      G7 C
Then Church of England's Glory,
                   G7         C
Another face of things was seen,
          F     G7 C
And I became a Tory.
   Am  G      Am      Em
Occasional conformists base,
     Am        G D7 G
I blamed their moderation,
         C                    G7    C
And thought the Church in danger was
      F  G7  C
By such prevarication.
```

```
        C                G7         C
When George in pudding time came o'er,
                  F         G7  C
And moderate men looked big, sir,
                    G7           C
My principles I changed once more,
          F      G7    C
And so became a Whig, sir.
    Am   G       Am Em
And thus preferment I procured
            Am     G    D7 G
From our new faith's defender,
          C           G7        C
And almost every day abjured
              F     G7 C
The Pope and the Pretender.
```

```
            C                  G7  C
The illustrious house of Hanover,
             F       G7  C
And Protestant succession,
                 G7        C
To these I do allegiance swear,
               F     G7  C
While they can keep possession.
       Am    G       Am Em
For in my faith and loyalty
       Am     G     D7  G
I never more will falter,
              C               G7      C
And George my lawful king shall be,
          F        G7 C
Until the times do alter.
```

# Ilkley Moor

Ilkley Moor is in Yorkshire. To venture out on Ilkley Moor baht 'at (without a hat) is surely to risk catching thy death of cold.

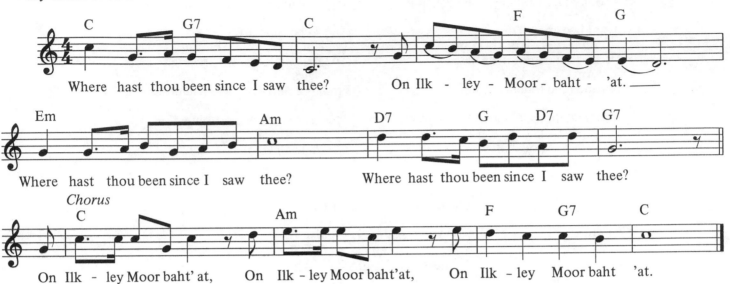

| C | G7 | C |
|---|---|---|
| I've been a-courting Mary Jane, | | |
| | F | G |
| On Ilkley Moor baht 'at. | | |
| Em | | Am |
| I've been a-courting Mary Jane, | | |
| D7 | G | D7 G |
| I've been a-courting Mary Jane. | | *Chorus* |

| C | G7 | C |
|---|---|---|
| Then worms will come and eat thee oop, | | |
| | F | G |
| On Ilkley Moor baht 'at. | | |
| Em | | Am |
| Then worms will come and eat thee oop, | | |
| D7 | G | D7 G |
| Then worms will come and eat thee oop. *Chorus* | | |

| C | G7 | C |
|---|---|---|
| Thou'll surely catch thy death of cold, | | |
| | F | G |
| On Ilkley Moor baht 'at. | | |
| Em | | Am |
| Thou'll surely catch thy death of cold, | | |
| D7 | G | D7 G |
| Thou'll surely catch thy death of cold. | | *Chorus* |

| C | G7 | C |
|---|---|---|
| Then dooks will come and eat oop worms, | | |
| | F | G |
| On Ilkley Moor baht 'at. | | |
| Em | | Am |
| Then dooks will come and eat oop worms, | | |
| D7 | G | D7 G |
| Then dooks will come and eat oop worms. *Chorus* | | |

| C | G7 | C |
|---|---|---|
| Then we shall have to bury thee, | | |
| | F | G |
| On Ilkley Moor baht 'at. | | |
| Em | | Am |
| Then we shall have to bury thee, | | |
| D7 | G | D7 G |
| Then we shall have to bury thee. | | *Chorus* |

| C | G7 | C |
|---|---|---|
| Then we will come and eat oop dooks, | | |
| | F | G |
| On Ilkley Moor baht 'at. | | |
| Em | | Am |
| Then we will come and eat oop dooks, | | |
| D7 | G | D7 G |
| Then we will come and eat oop dooks. *Chorus* | | |

| C | G7 | C |
|---|---|---|
| Then we will have thee back again, | | |
| | F | G |
| On Ilkley Moor baht 'at. | | |
| Em | | Am |
| Then we will have thee back again, | | |
| D7 | G | D7 G |
| Then we will have thee back again. | | *Chorus* |

# They're Moving Father's Grave

They're mov-ing fa-ther's grave to build a sew-er____ They're
shift-ing it re-gard-less of ex-pense. They're mov-ing his re-mains to
lay down nine-inch drains, to sat-is-fy some posh bloke's res-i-dence. Now
had the blood-y nerve to bug-ger up a Brit-ish work-man's grave ( a work-man's grave.)

```
          G                    D7              G                          D7
Now, what's the use of having a religion?     My father in his life was ne'er a quitter,
                                  G                                    G
For when you die your troubles never cease.   I'm sure that he'll not be a quitter now.
         Em                                          Em
When some high society crank needs a pipeline for his tank,   He'll put on a white sheet and haunt that privy seat,
   A7                        G♯° D7              A7                  G♯° D7
They won't let poor old father rest in peace.   And he'll only let them go when he'll allow.
```

```
                   G                              D7
       Oh, won't there be some pains of constipation!
                                              G
       And won't those poor old bastards rant and rave!
                   Em
       But they'll get what they deserve, for they had the bloody nerve
            D7                           G
       To bugger up a British workman's grave.
```

53

# The Keeper

The keep-er would a-hunt-ing go, And un-der his coat he
car-ried a bow, All for to shoot at a mer-ry lit-tle doe, A
*Chorus*
mong the leaves so— green, O. Jack-ie boy! Mas-ter! Sing ye well Ver-y well.
Hey down! Ho down! Der-ry, der-ry down. A-mong the leaves so—
green, O. To my hey down, down! To my ho down, down!
Hey down! Ho down! Der-ry, der-ry down, A-mong the leaves so— green, O.

|   |   |
|---|---|
| C      F  C<br>The first doe he shot at he missed:<br><br>           F    C<br>The second doe he trimmed he kissed.<br>                G7<br>The third doe went where nobody wist,<br>C      G7  C<br>Among the leaves so green, O.    *Chorus* | C      F  C<br>The fifth doe she did cross the brook;<br><br>                F    C<br>The keeper fetched her back with his crook;<br>                  G7<br>Where she is now you must go and look,<br>C      G7  C<br>Among the leaves so green, O.    *Chorus* |
| C      F  C<br>The fourth doe she did cross the plain;<br>           F  C<br>The keeper fetched her back again;<br>                G7<br>Where she is now she may remain<br>C      G7  C<br>Among the leaves so green, O.    *Chorus* | C      F  C<br>The sixth doe she ran over the plain;<br>                F    C<br>But he with his hounds did turn her again,<br>                      G7<br>And it's there he did hunt in a merry, merry vein<br>C      G7  C<br>Among the leaves so green, O.    *Chorus* |

# Geordie

Various Geordies have laid claims to this old ballad. During the minority of James VI of Scotland (1566–1625) — who later became James I of England — Sir George Gordon, of "the lawless and turbulent Gordons of Gight," had become too familiar with the laird of Bignet's lady, for which he was imprisoned and likely to lose his life, but for the timely interference of his wife, Lady Ann, who came to Edinborough to plead his cause. The incident related in the ballad has also been imputed to another Gordon — George Gordon (1514–1562), fourth earl of Huntly during the reign of Queen Mary. However, the reference to London in the song points toward a possible English origin. In Ritson's *Northumberland Garland* (1793), the ballad is described as "A lamentable ditty made upon the death of a worthy gentleman named George Stoole."

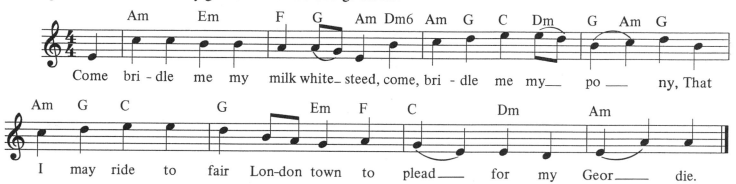

Come bri - dle me my milk white steed, come, bri - dle me my po — ny, That I may ride to fair Lon-don town to plead — for my Geor — die.

        Am     Em   F G Am
And when she entered in the hall,
Dm6      Am G  C Dm G Am G
There were lords and ladies plen - ty.
   Am G C     G    Em
Down on her knees she then did fall,
F  C     Dm    Am
To plead for the life of Geordie.

        Am    Em    F G Am
It's six pretty babes that I have got,
Dm6 Am   G  C Dm G Am G
The seventh lies in my bod - y.
   Am G C     G  Em
I'll freely part with them every one,
F     C     Dm   Am
If you'll spare me the life of Geordie.

       Am   Em   F G  Am
Then Geordie looked round the court,
Dm6 Am G  C Dm G Am G
And saw his dearest Pol - ly.
  Am  G  C    G  Em
He said, "My dear, you've come too late,
 F  C   Dm   Am
For I'm condemned already."

        Am    Em   F  G Am
Then the judge he looked down on him,
Dm6 Am   G  C Dm G Am G
And said, "I'm sorry for  thee.
   Am G C     G    Em
'Tis thine own confession hath hanged thee.
F     C     Dm Am
May the Lord have mercy on thee."

       Am   Em     F   G Am
O, Geordie stole nor cow nor calf,
Dm6  Am G C  Dm  G Am G
And he never murdered an - y.
      Am G C     G     Em
But he stole sixteen of the king's white steeds,
  F  C    Dm   Am
And sold them in Bohenny.

      Am   Em    F G   Am
Let Geordie hang in golden chains
Dm6  Am   G   C Dm G Am G
(His crimes were never man - y),
   Am  G  C    G   Em
Because he come of royal blood,
  F  C    Dm  Am
And courted a virtuous lady.

       Am Em    F     C
I wish I were in yonder grove,
 Dm6  Am G C Dm G Am  G
Where times I have been man - y.
     Am  G    C     G  Em
With my broad sword and my pistol too,
  F  C    Dm   Am
I'd fight for the life of Geordie.

# Under the Greenwood Tree

"Young lasses are never better pleased, than when, as upon a holiday, after evensong, they may meet their sweet-hearts, and dance about a May-pole, or in a Town-green, under a shady elm." (Robert Burton, *Anatomy of Melancholy,* 1621)

In_ sum - mer time, when flow'rs do spring,_ And birds sit on each tree,____ Let_
Lords and knights say what they will,__ Theres no so gay as we._____ There's
Will and Moll and Har - ry and Doll, And Tom and bon-ny' Bet - tee, Oh!_____
how they do jerk it. Ca - per and firk it, Un - der the green - wood tree._____

Chorus
In_ Sum -mer time when flow'rs do spring_And birds sit on each tree,____ Let_ we, _____
Lords and knights say what they will, Theres none so gay as

G
Our music is a little pipe,
D7              G
That can so sweetly play.
                    Em
We hire Old Hal from Whitsuntide
D7            G
'Til latter Lammas-day.
A7    D            D7  G
On Sabbath days and holy-days
    Em              Am
After evening prayers comes he;
D7  G        D7    G7    C  G
And then we do skip it, caper and trip it,
    D        A7      D  D7
Under the greenwood tree.          *Chorus*

G
"Come play us 'Adam and Eve,'" says Dick;
        D7              G
"What's that?" says little Pipe.
                            Em
"'The Beginning of the World,'" quoth Dick,
            D7        G
"For we are dancing ripe."
A7    D              D7    G
"Is't that you call? Then have at all—"
    Em              Am
He played with merry glee;
D7      G        D7    G7    C  G
O then we did skip it, caper and trip it,
    D        A7      D  D7
Under the greenwood tree.          *Chorus*

# Liliburlero

In 1688 Thomas Wharton, lord-lieutenant of Ireland, wrote this famous political ballad (to a tune composed the previous year by Henry Purcell). It satirized the Irish Jacobite Richard Talbot, Earl Tyrconnell, who had entered into intrigues for handing Ireland over to the king of France in order to secure the interest of his fellow Roman Catholics. It got to be known as the song which "sang James II out of three kingdoms." During the American Civil War, Francis James Child, author of the monumental work *The English and Scottish Popular Ballads,* borrowed this tune for another biting satire, "Overtures from Richmond," which ridiculed Jefferson Davis and the Confederacy.

D          A7
Ho, by my soul, it is a Talbot;
  D   G D A7   D
  Lilli burlero bullen ala.
            A7
And he will cut all the English throat,
  D   G D A7 D
  Lilli burlero bullen ala. *Chorus*


*Verses follow the above pattern*


  D                 A7
Though, by my soul, the English do prate,
  D                      A7
The law's on their side and the devil knows what. *Chorus*

  D                 A7
But if Dispense do come from the Pope,
  D                      A7
We'll hang Magna Carta and themselves on a rope. *Chorus*

  D                 A7
And the good Talbot is now made a Lord.
  D                      A7
And with his brave lads he's coming aboard. *Chorus*

  D                 A7
Who all in France have taken a swear,
  D                      A7
That they will have no Protestant heir. *Chorus*


D                    A7
O but why does he stay behind?
D                            A7
Ho, by my soul, 'tis a Protestant wind. *Chorus*


D                         A7
Now that Tyrconnel is come ashore,
  D                       A7
And we shall have Commissions galore. *Chorus*


D                       A7
And he that will not go to the Mass,
D                           A7
Shall be turned out and look like an ass. *Chorus*


D                       A7
Now, now the hereticks all will go down,
D                            A7
By Christ and St. Patrick's the nation's our own. *Chorus*


D                          A7
There was an old prophecy found in a bog,
D                              A7
That our land would be ruled by an ass and a dog. *Chorus*


D                            A7
So now this old prophecy's coming to pass,
D                            A7
For James is the dog and Tyrconnel's the ass. *Chorus*

# Tobacco's But an Indian Weed

In *The Marrow of Complements* (1654) is a poem entitled "Meditations on Tobacco" by George Withers, which begins:

> Why should we so much despise
> So good and wholesome an exercise
> As, early and late to meditate?
> Thus think, and drink tobacco.

The pros and cons of smoking (or "drinking," since the smoke was swallowed) had been raging since the introduction of tobacco into England in 1565. By 1699, Withers' poem had been set to music (in *Pills to Purge Melancholy*), with the first verse altered to express the anti-smokers' point of view.

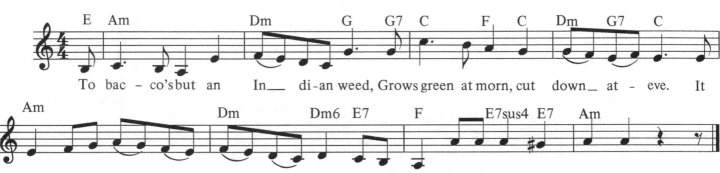

To bac - co's but an In__ di-an weed, Grows green at morn, cut down__ at - eve. It

shows our de-cay__ we __ are __ but __ clay: Think of this when you smoke to bac - co.

        E   Am          Dm  G
The pipe that is so lily-white,
        G7  C    F  C Dm G7 C
Wherein so many take delight,
        Am          F
Gone with a touch;
        Dm   Dm6
Man's life is such,
        E7       F              E7/4 E7 Am
Think on this, when you smoke tobacco.

        E   Am          Dm  G
The pipe that is so foul within,
        G7   C     F C  Dm    G7 C
Shews how the soul is stained with sin;
        Am   F
It doth require
        Dm   Dm6
The purging fire.
        E7       F              E7/4 E7 Am
Think on this, when you smoke tobacco.

        E   Am          Dm  G
The ashes that are left behind,
        G7   C     F C Dm G7 C
Do serve to put us all in mind,
            Am  F
That unto dust,
        Dm      Dm6
Return we must.
        E7       F              E7/4 E7 Am
Think on this, when you smoke tobacco.

        E   Am            Dm  G
The smoke that doth so high ascend;
        G7   C     F  C   Dm G7 C
Shows that our life must have an end;
            Am   F
The vapour's gone,
        Dm   Dm6
Man's life is done.
        E7       F              E7/4 E7 Am
Think on this, when you smoke tobacco.

# The Roast Beef of Old England

When might - y roast beef was the Eng -lish man's food, It en - no - bled our hearts and en -
riched o - ur blood; Our sol – diers were brave, and our court - iers were good
Oh, the roast beef of old Eng — land! And oh, for old Eng -land's roast beef!_____

      A         E       A       E
But since we have learn'd from effeminate France
      B7     E    B7    E
To eat their ragouts, as well as to dance,
      D         A  F#7
We are fed up with nothing but vain complaisance. *Chorus*

      A         E       A       E
Our fathers of old were robust, stout and strong,
      B7     E    B7    E
And kept open house, with good cheer all day long,
      D         A  F#7
Which made their plump tenants rejoice in this song. *Chorus*

      A         E       A       E
When good Queen Elizabeth sat on the throne,
      B7     E    B7    E
Ere coffee and tea, and such slip-slops were known,
      D         A  F#7
The world was in terror if e'en she did frown. *Chorus*

      A         E       A       E
In *those* days, if fleets did presume on the main,
      B7     E  B7    E
They seldom or never return'd back again;
      D         A  F#7
As witness the vaunting Armada of Spain. *Chorus*

      A         E       A       E
Oh, then we had stomachs to eat and to fight,
      B7     E    B7    E
And when wrongs were cooking, to set ourselves right;
      D         A  F#7
But now we're a-hm!—I could, but good night. *Chorus*

# Saddle to Rags

"This ballad appears to have been very popular in the days when highwaymen were a feature in the travels of our ancestors. The present version of the ballad . . . is taken from a scarce little song-book entitled, *The Manchester Songster,* 1792, there named *The Yorkshire Farmer. . . .*" (Frank Kidson, *Supplement to Old English Popular Music,* 1893)

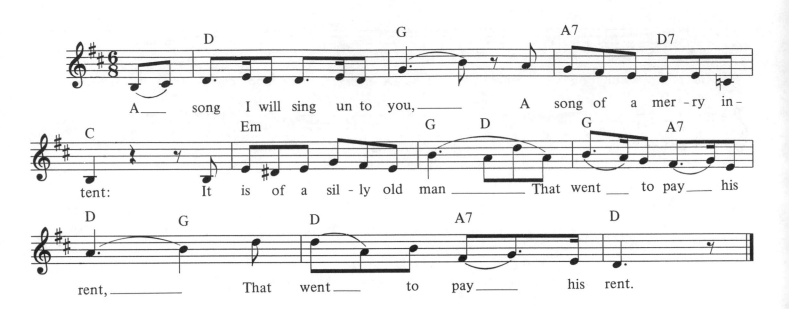

A___ song I will sing un to you, ___ A song of a mer-ry in-tent: It is of a sil-ly old man ___ That went ___ to pay ___ his rent, ___ That went ___ to pay ___ his rent.

|                          |                          |
|--------------------------|--------------------------|
|    D            G |    D            G |
| And as he was riding along, | So as they were riding along, |
|    A7   D7     G |    A7   D7     G |
| A-riding along the highway, | And going down a steep hill, |
|   Em        G       D |   Em        G       D |
| A gentleman thief steps before the old man, | The gentleman thief slipped before the old man, |
|     G     A7     D G |     G     A7     D G |
| And thus unto him he did say, | And quickly he bid him stand still, |
|    D    A7      D |    D    A7      D |
| And thus unto him he did say: | And quickly he bid him stand still. |
| | |
|      D               G |      D               G |
| "My friend, how dare you ride alone, | The old man, however, being cunning, |
|    A7    D7      G |    A7    D7      G |
| For so many thieves there now be, | As in his world there are many; |
|   Em        G D |   Em        G       D |
| If any should but light on you, | He threw the saddle right over the hedge, |
|     G     A7     D G |     G     A7        D G |
| They'd rob you of all your money, | Saying, "Fetch it if thou wouldst have any," |
|    D    A7      D |    D    A7      D |
| They'd rob you of all your money." | Saying, "Fetch it if thou wouldst have any." |
| | |
|      D               G |      D               G |
| "If that they should light upon me, | The thief being so greedy of money, |
|    A7     D7      G |    A7    D7      G |
| I'm sure they'd be very ill-sped; | He thought that of it there'd been bags, |
|   Em        G D |   Em        G       D |
| For, to tell you the truth, my kind sir, | Whipt out a rusty old sword, |
|     G     A7     D G |     G     A7     D G |
| In my saddle my money I've hid, | And chopped the saddle to rags, |
|    D    A7      D |    D    A7      D |
| In my saddle my money I've hid." | And chopped the saddle to rags. |

```
        D                              G
The old man put his foot in the stirrup,
        A7    D7       G
And presently he got astride.
   Em                 G  D
He put the thief's horse to the gallop,
        G          A7       D  G
You need not bid the old man ride,
        D          A7      D
You need not bit the old man ride.


        D                        G
"Nay, stay! Nay, stay!" says the thief,
        A7    D7              G
  "And half the money thou shalt have."
   Em                G  D
"Nay, by my troth," says the old man,
     G            A7       D  G
  "For once I have cheated a knave,
   D          A7       D
For once I have cheated a knave."
```

```
        D                        G
And so the old man rode along,
        A7       D7       G
  And went with a merry devotion,
   Em                    G  D
Saying, "If ever I live to get home,
        G          A7        D  G
  T'will enlarge my daughter's portion,
        D          A7         D
T'will enlarge my daughter's portion.


        D                        G
And having arrived at home,
        A7       D7       G
  And got there with merry intent;
   Em                        G  D
Says he, "Landlord, show me a room,
        G          A7        D  G
  And I'll pay you your half-year's rent,
        D          A7       D
And I'll pay you your half-year's rent."
```

```
        D                        G
They opened the thief's portmanteau,
        A7       D7       G
  And from it they took out so bold,
   Em                G  D
A hundred pounds in silver,
        G      A7       D  G
  And a hundred pounds in gold,
        D              A7
And a hundred pounds in gold.
```

# It's the Same the Whole World Over

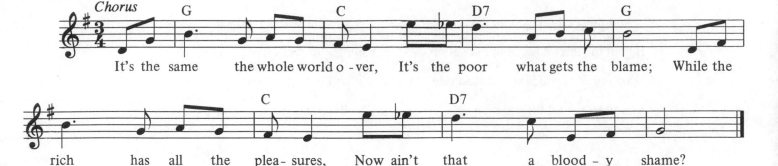

*Chorus*

It's the same the whole world o-ver, It's the poor what gets the blame; While the rich has all the plea-sures, Now ain't that a blood-y shame?

|  | G | C |
|---|---|---|
She was poor, but she was honest,
|  | D7 | G |
Pure unstained was her fame,
|  |  | C |
Till a country squire come courting,
|  | D7 | G |
And the poor girl lost her name. *Chorus*

|  | G | C |
So she went away to London,
|  | D7 | G |
Just to hide her guilty shame,
|  |  | C |
There she met an Army Chaplain -
|  | D7 | G |
Once again she lost her name. *Chorus*

|  | G | C |
Hear him as he jaws the Tommies,
|  | D7 | G |
Warning of the devil's flame.
|  |  | C |
With her whole heart she had trusted,
|  | D7 | G |
But again she lost her name. *Chorus*

|  | G | C |
So she settled down in London,
|  | D7 | G |
Sinking deeper in her shame,
|  |  | C |
Till she met a labor leader
|  | D7 | G |
And again she lost her name. *Chorus*

|  | G | C |
Now he's in the House of Commons,
|  | D7 | G |
Making laws to put down crime,
|  |  | C |
While the victim of his pleasure
|  | D7 | G |
Walks the street each night in shyme. *Chorus*

|  | G | C |
Then there came a bloated bishop.
|  | D7 | G |
Marriage was the tale he told.
|  |  | C |
There was no one else to take her,
|  | D7 | G |
So she sold her soul for gold. *Chorus*

|  | G | C |
In that rich man's arms she fluttered
|  | D7 | G |
Like a bird with broken wing.
|  |  | C |
First he loved her, then he left her,
|  | D7 | G |
And the poor girl got no ring. *Chorus*

|  | G | C |
See that girl outside the poorhouse
|  | D7 | G |
Selling matches by the box,
|  |  | C |
While that swell from high society
|  | D7 | G |
Hands out doses of the pox! *Chorus*

|  | G | C |
In a cottage down in Sussex
|  | D7 | G |
Lives her parents old and lame,
|  |  | C |
And they drink the wine she sends them,
|  | D7 | G |
But they never speaks her name. *Chorus*

|  | G | C |
In their poor and humble dwelling,
|  | D7 | G |
There her grieving parents live.
|  |  | C |
Sipping champagne as she sends them,
|  | D7 | G |
But they never can forgive. *Chorus*

# The Husband with No Courage in Him

"Here is one of those hidden love songs of Britain, a song collected several times yet never considered fit to print. In it, a wife laments the sexual shortcomings of her husband. . . . The song is in unusual meter, considered by some to be Scottish, though, in fact, the song has been collected most often in the far south of England, in Somerset and Dorset." (A. L. Lloyd)

As— I walked out one sum-mer's day, To view the fields and the liz-ards spring-in,' I— saw two maid-ens stand-in' by, And— one of them her hands was wring-in,' And— all of her con-ver-sa-tion— was, "My hus-band's got no cour-age in him. Oh dear, no. Oh dear, no. My— hus-band's got no cour-age in him. Oh dear, no."

Dm    Em   Am
All sorts of meat I do preserve,
Dm     Em
All sorts of drink that's fittin' for him,
Dm    Em   Am
Both oyster pies and rhubarb, too,
Dm    Em   Am
But nothing will put courage in him.    *Chorus*

Dm    Em   Am
It's seven long years I've made his bed,
Dm    Em
And seven years I've laid agin him,
Dm      Em   Am
And this morn I rose with my maidenhead,
Dm     Em   Am
Now, that shows he's got no courage in him.   *Chorus*

Dm      Em   Am
Come, pretty maids, where'er you be,
Dm    Em
Don't wed a man before you try him,
Dm    Em   Am
Lest you should sing a song like me,
Dm    Em   Am
My husband's got no courage in him.    *Chorus*

Dm      Em    Am
I wish to God that he were dead,
Dm    Em
And in his grave I'd quickly lay him,
Dm    Em   Am
Then I would try another one
Dm    Em   Am
That had a little courage in him.    *Chorus*

           F        C   Am
*Final Chorus:*   Then I would try another one
           Dm      Em
           That had a little courage in him,
           Am        D
           Oh dear, yes, oh dear, yes.
           Dm      Em   Am
           That had a little courge in him,
           D     Am
           Oh dear, yes.

# Me Father's a Lawyer in England

Me fa-ther's a law-yer in Eng-land, Me moth-er's a jus-tice of peace, Me sis-ter's a Shak-er and an ap-ple pie bak-er, She makes them of tal-ler and grease.

*Chorus*

To-me-fang, to-me-fang, fang-o-lear-y. To-me-fang, to-me-fang, fang-o-lay, To-me hoot-te-toot, toot-te-toot, lar-ry. To-me-whack, fal-dee did-dle al-a-day, To-me-whack, fal-dee-did-dle al-de-day. ————

Me father is a hedger and ditcher, (E B7 E)
Me mother does nothing but spin; (A)
Me sister is a Shaker and an apple pie maker. (E A)
O how the money comes in. (B7 E) *Chorus*

Me wife she is dirty, she's nasty; (E B7 E)
She is lousy and itchy and black, (A)
She's a divil for fighting and scolding; (E A)
Her tongue it goes clickety-clack. (B7 E) *Chorus*

My father's an apple pie baker, (E B7 E)
My mother makes synthetic gin, (A)
My sister sells sin to the sailors, (E A)
My God, how the money rolls in. (B7 E) *Chorus*

My brother's a street missionary, (E B7 E)
He saves little girlies from sin, (A)
He'll save you a blonde for a shilling, (E A)
My God, how the money rolls in. (B7 E) *Chorus*

# Rap Tap Tap

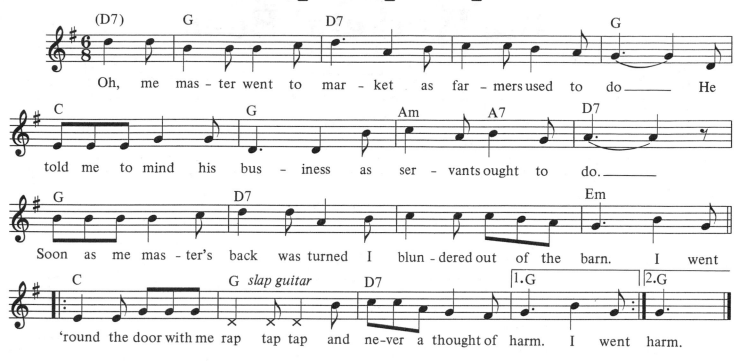

Oh, me mas-ter went to mar-ket as far-mers used to do ——— He
told me to mind his bus-iness as ser-vants ought to do. ———
Soon as me mas-ter's back was turned I blun-dered out of the barn. I went
'round the door with me rap tap tap and ne-ver a thought of harm. I went harm.

```
        G                D7                        G
Soon as me missus heard me, she asked me to step in.
      C          G     Am  A7      D7
I told her I felt so weary, so she give me some gin.
        G                D7              Em
She ordered me to drink it and devil a word to say.
          C          G          D7              G
She knew so well me rap tap tap, upstairs we went straightway. (2)


            G               D7                   G
We lay a-sporting on the bed for half an hour or more,
         C              G      Am  A7        D7
The missus liked the game so well, I thought she'd never give o'er.
        G               D7                      Em
"You've won my heart, young man," she said, "My husband's not for me.
        C            G           D7          G
"For he can't come with his rap tap tap not half as well as thee. (2)


          G            D7                        G
Soon as me master he come home he asked what I'd done.
      C              G       Am  A7     D7
I told him I'd minded his business as if it were my own.
        G             D7                        Em
Then he give to me some beer, my boys, for, indeed, he didn't know
        C              G            D7              G
That I'd been there with my rap tap tap, if he did he'd a-never done so.  (2)
```

# The Man Who Waters the Workers' Beer

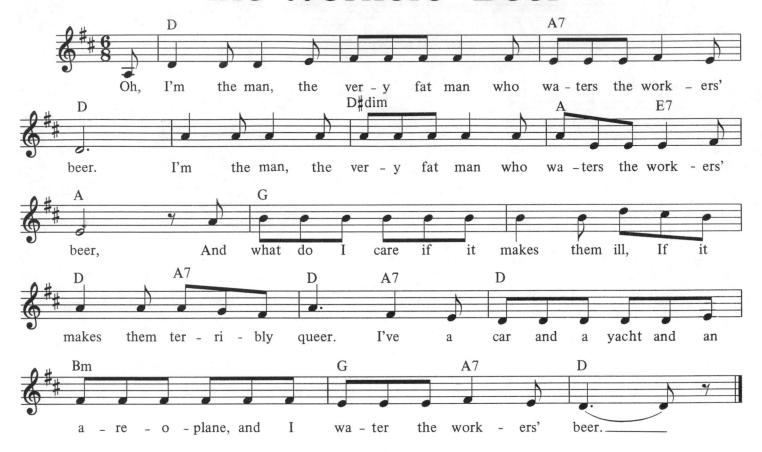

Oh, I'm the man, the ver-y fat man who wa-ters the work-ers' beer. I'm the man, the ver-y fat man who wa-ters the work-ers' beer, And what do I care if it makes them ill, If it makes them ter-ri-bly queer. I've a car and a yacht and an a-re-o-plane, and I wa-ter the work-ers' beer.

        D                                   A7           D
Now, when I waters the workers' beer I puts in strychinine,

               D♯dim     A     E7  A
Some methylated spirits and a drop of kerosene;

         G                               D       A7     D
But since a brew so terribly strong might make them feel terribly queer,

A7  D               Bm          G      A7   D
I reaches my hand for the water tap and waters the workers' beer. *Chorus*

          D                                   A7         D
Now, a drop of beer is good for a man when he's tired and thirsty and hot.

             D♯dim           A   E7  A
I sometimes takes a drop myself - from a very special lot.

         G                             D    A7    D
But a fat and healthy working class is the thing that I most fear,

A7  D               Bm          G    A7     D
So I reaches my hand for the water tap and waters the workers' beer. *Chorus*

          D                                A7         D
Now, ladies fair beyond compare, and be ye maid or wife,

             D♯dim           A   E7  D
Sometimes lend a thought to one who leads a sorry life.

         G                             D   A7    D
The water rates are shockingly high and malt is terribly dear

A7  D               Bm          G    A7     D
And there isn't the profit there used to be in watering workers' beer. *Chorus*

66

# Charlie Mopps

Chorus:
Oh, he oughta been an admiral, a sultan or a king;
And to his praises we should always sing.
Oh, look what he has done for us, he's filled us up with cheer,
Lord bless Charlie Mopps - the man who invented beer (beer, beer, diddley. . .)


The Abbey, The Connaught, The Hole In The wall, as well
One thing you can sure, it's Charlie's beer they sell.
So come on all you lucky lads, at ten o'clock she stops,
For five short seconds, remember Charlie Mopps.


Spoken: One. . . two. . . three. . .four. . .five. . . . Chorus


A bushel of hops and a barrel of malt and stir around with a stick.
The sort of lubrication to make your engine tick.
Twenty pints of wallop a day will keep away the quacks
It's only fourpence ha' penny a pint and a shilling and tuppence in tax.


Spoken: Shame. . . shame. . . shame. . . Chorus

67

# The Coal Owner and the Pitman's Wife

This ballad was found among a collection of papers relating to a strike in Lancaster in 1844. It was written by a miner named William Hornsby.

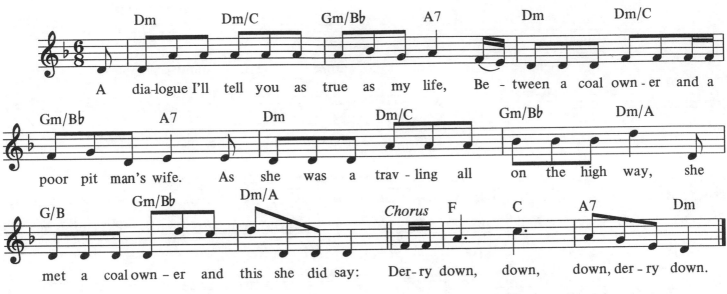

     Dm      Dm/C   Gm/B♭  A7
"Good morning, Lord Firedamp," this woman she said,
     Dm      Dm/C   Gm/B♭  A7
"I'll do you no harm, sir, so don't be afraid.
     Dm      Dm/C   Gm/B♭  Dm/A
If you'd been where I'd been the most of my life,
      G/B     Gm/B♭   Dm/A
You wouldn't turn pale at a poor pitman's wife." *Chorus*

     Dm      Dm/C     Gm/B♭  A7
"Then where do you come from?" the owner, he cries.
Dm      Dm/C   Gm/B♭  A7
"I come from hell," the woman replies.
     Dm      Dm/C     Gm/B♭  Dm/A
"If you come from hell, then come tell me right plain
G/B     Gm/B♭  Dm/A
How you contrived to get out again." *Chorus*

     Dm      Dm/C  Gm/B♭  A7
"Aye, the way I got out, the truth I will tell;
      Dm      Dm/C  Gm/B♭    A7
They're turning the poor folk all out of hell.
Dm      Dm/C    Gm/B♭  Dm/A
This to make room for the rich wicked race,
     G/B     Gm/B♭  Dm/A
For there is a great number of them in that place." *Chorus*

     Dm      Dm/C   Gm/B♭   A7
"And the coal owners' selves is the next on command
     Dm     Dm/C  Gm/B♭  A7
To arrive into hell, as I understand,
     Dm      Dm/C   Gm/B♭  Dm/A
For I heard the old Devil say, as I came out,
     G/B     Gm/B♭  Dm/A
The coal owners all had received their rout." *Chorus*

        Dm      Dm/C Gm/B♭   A7
"Then how does the old Devil behave in that place?"
      Dm     Dm/C    Gm/B♭   A7
"Oh sir, he is cruel to the rich wicked race.
     Dm      Dm/C     Gm/B♭  Dm/A
He is far more uncrueller than you can suppose,
     G/B     Gm/B♭  Dm/A
Even like a mad bull with a ring through his nose." *Chorus*

       Dm      Dm/C   Gm/B♭   A7
"Good woman," says he, "I must bid you farewell.
      Dm     Dm/C  Gm/B♭  A7
You give me a dismal account about hell.
     Dm     Dm/C    Gm/B♭  Dm/A
If this be all true that you say unto me,
        G/B     Gm/B♭     Dm/A
I'll be home like a whippet and with my poor men agree." *Chorus*

        Dm      Dm/C   Gm/B♭    A7
"If you be a coal owner, sir, take my advice,
      Dm      Dm/C    Gm/B♭    A7
Agree with your men and give them a full price.
      Dm   Dm/C Gm/B♭  Dm/A
For if you do not, I know very well,
     G/B     Gm/B♭  Dm/A
You'll be in great danger of going to hell." *Chorus*

# Pit Boots

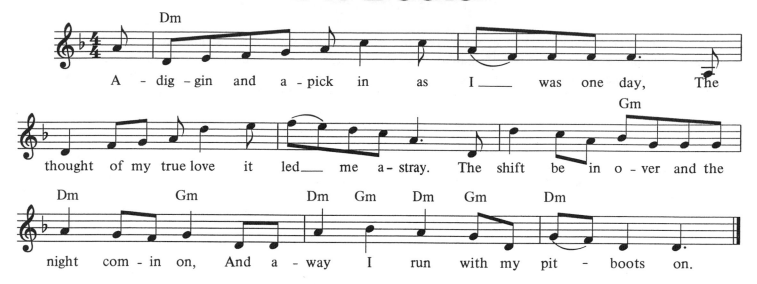

A - dig - gin and a - pick in as I _____ was one day, The
thought of my true love it led ___ me a - stray. The shift be in o - ver and the
night com - in on, And a - way I run with my pit - boots on.

Dm
I went to my love's window cryin: "Are you in bed?"

The minute that she heard me, she lifted up her head.
       Gm         Dm       Gm
She lifted up her head cryin: "Oh, is that John?"
   Dm Gm Dm Gm    Dm
"Indeed it's me with me pit boots on."

Dm
She come to the door and invited me in.

"Draw up to the fire and warm your skin."
       Gm         Dm         Gm
The bedroom door it opened and the blanket it turned down,
   Dm Gm Dm Gm    Dm
And I rolled into bed with me pit boots on.

Dm
We tossed and we tumbled until the break of day,

Not thinkin' of the hours that we had passed away,
       Gm         Dm       Gm
Till my love she sat up, cryin: "Oh, what have I done?"
    Dm Gm Dm Gm   Dm
The baby will come with his pit boots on!

Dm
I chastised my love for talkin' so wild.

"You silly young girl, you will never have a child,
       Gm         Dm       Gm
For all that we done it was just a bit of fun."
    Dm Gm Dm Gm   Dm
But away I run with me pit boots on.

           Dm
Come all you young maidens wherever that you be,

Beware of them colliers who are single and free,
         Gm       Dm     Gm
For their hearts do run light and their minds do run young.
      Dm Gm   Dm Gm   Dm
So look out for the fellows with the pit boots on!

# The Durham Lockout

"A most remarkable colliery balladeer was Tommy Armstrong (1848–1919) whose long working life from the age of eight was spent in the pits around Tanfield, Co. Durham. A small man with a large thirst and fourteen children, Armstrong wrote a vast number of songs of mining life which he had printed on broadsides and hawked in the local pubs to provide himself with beer money. Besides these, his output includes many strike songs and disaster ballads written to raise funds for the union or for the relief of widows and orphans. Most of his strike songs belong to the militant years between 1888 and 1893 when the membership of the Miners' Federation grew from 36,000 to over 200,000. The great Durham lock-out began in March, 1892. A fall in coal prices led the owners to propose a 10% wage reduction. The men refused and were locked out. After six weeks, with their families almost starving, the men declared they would accept the wage-cut, but now the owners demanded 13½%. Armstrong's ballad was written at this point, at the beginning of May, 1892. The men refused; the strike dragged on; eventually a 10% reduction was agreed to. (From *The Iron Muse, A Panorama of Industrial Folk Song*, a 1962 Topic recording, sung by Bob Davenport)

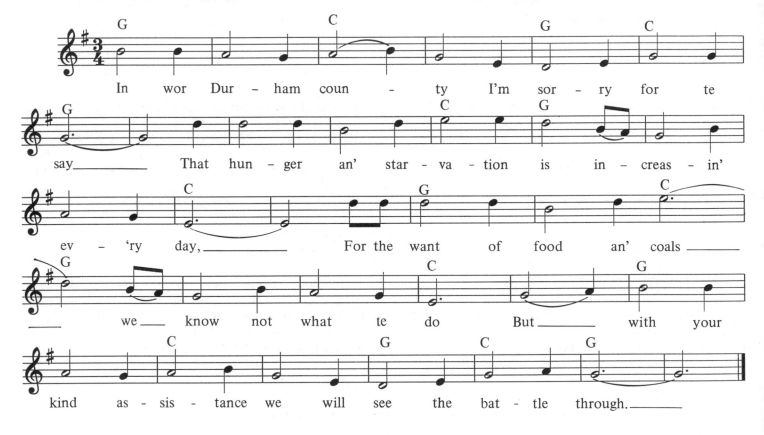

I need not state the reason why we've been browt se low.

The masters have behaved unkind, which everyone will know.

Because we won't lie doon an' let them treat us as they like,

Te punish us they've stopped the pits an' caused the present strike.


The pulley-wheels have ceased te move which went se swift around.

The horses an' the ponies tae are browt from undergroond.

Wor work is taken from us an' they care not if we die,

For they can eat the best o' food an' drink the best when dry.

```
        G              C            G    C    G
The miner an' his wife tae each mornin have te roam
             C           G                     C
To seek for bread te feed the hungry little ones at home.
        G            C      G                         C
The flour barrel is empty noo, their true an' faithful friend,
        G            C          G      C  G
Which makes the thoosands wish teday the strike was at an end.

        G              C           G    C      G
Well, let them stand or let them lie or do whatever they choose;
               C    G                    C
Te give them thorteen and a half we ever shall refuse.
        G            C  G                        C
They're always willin te receive but not inclined te give,
        G          C      G    C  G
An' very soon they won't allow a workin' man te live.
```

# Handsome Molly

I wish I was in Lon-don, or some oth-er sea-port town, I'd
set my-self on a steam-ship and sail the o-cean 'round.

G
While sailing 'round the ocean,

       D
While sailing 'round the sea,

I'd think of handsome Molly
C       G
Wherever she may be.


G
Do you remember, Molly,

       D
You gave your right hand?

You said if ever you'd marry
C           G
That I would be your man.


        G
I'll go down to the river

             D
When everyone's asleep,

I'll think of handsome Molly
    C           G
And then sit down and weep.


          G
Now you have broke your promise,

                D
Go home with who you please,

While my poor heart is aching,
    C           G
Here lying at your ease.


          G
Now, Molly's fair and handsome,

              D
Her hands are long and small,

They say she is good-natured
    C           G
And that's the best of all.
```
```

# The House Carpenter

Based upon a Roxburghe ballad sheet on Thackeray's list of 1685, called "A Warning to Married Women."

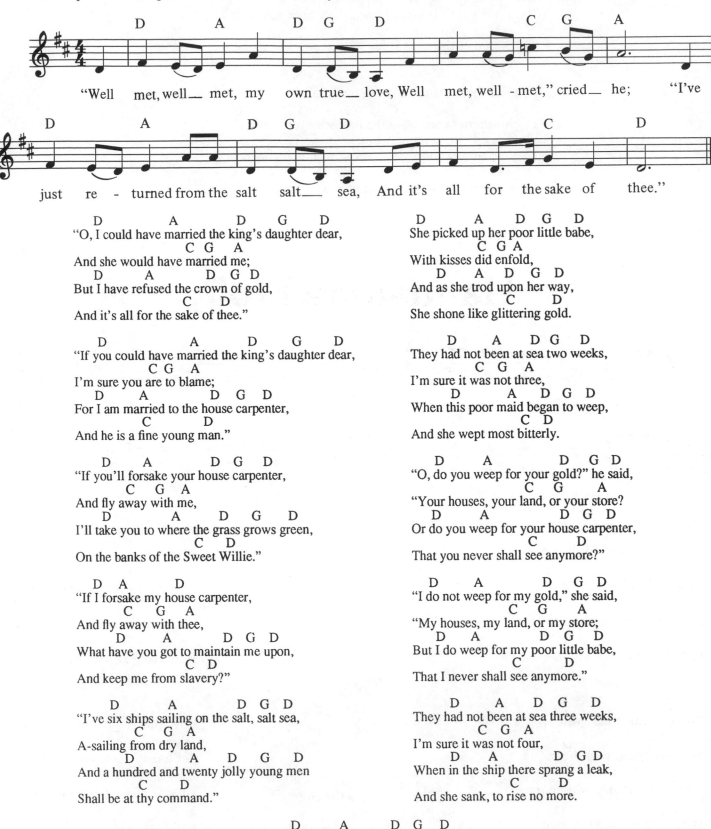

"Well met, well met, my own true love, Well met, well-met," cried he; "I've just re-turned from the salt salt sea, And it's all for the sake of thee."

     D     A     D G D
"O, I could have married the king's daughter dear,
     C G   A
And she would have married me;
     D     A     D G D
But I have refused the crown of gold,
     C   D
And it's all for the sake of thee."

     D     A     D G D
"If you could have married the king's daughter dear,
     C G   A
I'm sure you are to blame;
     D     A     D G D
For I am married to the house carpenter,
     C   D
And he is a fine young man."

     D     A     D G D
"If you'll forsake your house carpenter,
     C G   A
And fly away with me,
     D     A     D G D
I'll take you to where the grass grows green,
     C   D
On the banks of the Sweet Willie."

     D A     D
"If I forsake my house carpenter,
     C G   A
And fly away with thee,
     D     A     D G D
What have you got to maintain me upon,
     C   D
And keep me from slavery?"

     D     A     D G D
"I've six ships sailing on the salt, salt sea,
     C G   A
A-sailing from dry land,
     D     A     D G D
And a hundred and twenty jolly young men
     C   D
Shall be at thy command."

     D     A     D G D
She picked up her poor little babe,
     C G   A
With kisses did enfold,
     D     A     D G D
And as she trod upon her way,
     C   D
She shone like glittering gold.

     D     A     D G D
They had not been at sea two weeks,
     C G   A
I'm sure it was not three,
     D     A     D G D
When this poor maid began to weep,
     C   D
And she wept most bitterly.

     D     A     D G D
"O, do you weep for your gold?" he said,
     C G   A
"Your houses, your land, or your store?
     D     A     D G D
Or do you weep for your house carpenter,
     C   D
That you never shall see anymore?"

     D     A     D G D
"I do not weep for my gold," she said,
     C G   A
"My houses, my land, or my store;
     D A     D G D
But I do weep for my poor little babe,
     C   D
That I never shall see anymore."

     D     A     D G D
They had not been at sea three weeks,
     C G   A
I'm sure it was not four,
     D     A     D G D
When in the ship there sprang a leak,
     C   D
And she sank, to rise no more.

     D     A     D G D
"Farewell, farewell, my own true love,
     C G   A
Farewell, farewell," cried she;
     D     A     D G D
"O, I have deserted my house carpenter,
     C   D
For a grave in the depths of the sea."

# The Eddystone Light

The Eddystone rocks lie about 14 miles off Plymouth. Four lighthouses have been constructed on these rocks: Winstanley's Tower, completed in 1698 and swept away in November 1703; Ruyard's Tower, completed in 1709 and destroyed by fire in 1755; Smeaton's Tower, completed in 1759 and dismantled when the Douglass Tower was completed in 1882. Probably the keeper in question exercised his functions either in the latter years of the Smeaton Tower or the early years of the Douglass Tower.

My father was the keep-er of the Ed-dy-stone Light, And he slept with a mer-maid one fine night. From this un-ion there came three. Two lit-tle fish-es and the oth-er was me.

*Chorus*

Yo ho ho, the wind blows free. Oh, for the life on the roll-ing sea.

C
One night as I was a-trimming of the glim,
    F    G7        C
And a-singing a verse from the evening hymn,

A voice from the starboard shouted, "Ahoy!"
    F        G7     C
And there was my mother a-sitting on a buoy.   *Chorus*

             C
"Oh, what has become of my children three?"
    F    G7     C
My mother then she said to me.

"One was exhibited as a talking fish,
         F     G7     C
And the other was served on a chafing dish."   *Chorus*

            C
Then the phosphorous flashed in her seaweed hair,
    F    G7      C
I looked again and mother wasn't there.

But a voice came echoing out through the night.
    F    G7      C
"To hell with the keeper of the Eddystone Light!"   *Chorus*

# Handsome Cabin Boy

The story of the woman who dons men's clothes and goes to sea is a favorite in British sea-song tradition. Perhaps a few such occurrences inspired ballad-makers to expand on the almost limitless possibilities of the theme. This version of the song is somewhat unusual due to the presence of the captain's wife — leading one to suspect that she was written into the song to provide some justification for the captain's philandering.

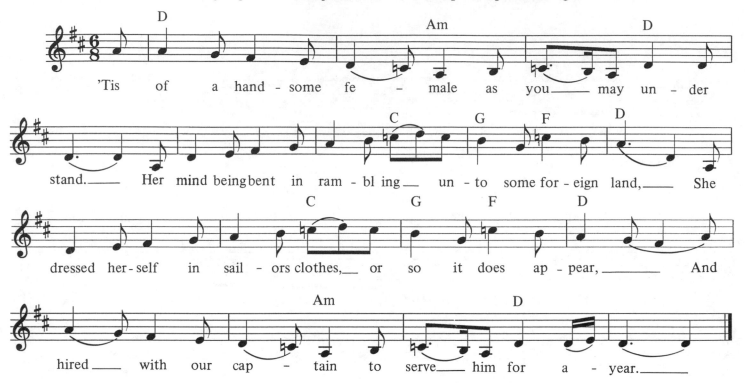

The captain's wife she being on board, she seem-ed in great joy,
To see her husband had engaged such a handsome cabin boy,
And now and then she'd slip in a kiss and she would have liked to toy,
But the captain found the secret of the handsome cabin boy.

Her cheeks were red and rosy and her hair hung in its curls,
The sailors often smiled and said he looks just like a girl.
But eating the captain's biscuits, their color didn't destroy,
And the waist did swell on pretty Nell, the handsome cabin boy.

'Twas in the Bay of Biscay our gallant ship did plow,
One night among the sailors was a fearful scurrying row,
They tumbled from their hammocks for their sleep it did destroy,
And swore about the groaning of the handsome cabin boy.

```
     D              Am           D
Oh, doctor, oh dear doctor, the cabin boy did cry,
                          C    G    F     D
My time has come, I am undone and I must surely die.
                          C    G   F    D
The doctor come a-running and smiled at the fun,
                          Am              D
To think a sailor lad should have a daughter or a son.


     D                        Am            D
The sailors when they heard the joke, they all did stand and stare,
                          C      G    F    D
The child belonged to none of them they solemnly did swear.
                          C     G    F      D
The captain's wife she looked at him and said, "I wish you joy,
                          Am               D
For it's either you or I betrayed the handsome cabin boy."


     D                      Am           D
Then each man took his tot of rum, and drunk success to trade,
                          C       G    F     D
And likewise to the cabin boy who was neither man nor maid.
                          C     G    F    D
Here's hopin' the wars don't rise again, our sailors to destroy,
                          Am                    D
And here's hoping for a jolly lot more like the handsome cabin boy.
```

# High Barbaree

The coastal population of northern Africa has in past ages been addicted to piratical attacks on shores and shipping of Europe opposite. The conquest of Granada by the Catholic sovereigns of Spain drove many Moors into exile. They revenged themselves by piratical attacks on the Spanish coast. The first half of the 17th century may be described as the flowering time of the Barbary pirates. More than 20,000 captives were said to be imprisoned in Algiers alone. In 1655 the British admiral Robert Blake was sent out on a major punitive expedition. A long series of similar expeditions was undertaken by the British fleet during the reign of Charles II. In the 1680s the French bombarded Algiers, but the piracy continued into the 19th century. The "Marines' Hymn" ("From the halls of Montezuma to the shores of Tripoli . . .") commemorates American involvement in 1801–05 and again in 1815. In 1824 another British fleet under Admiral Sir Harry Neal had again to bombard Algiers. The great pirate city was not in fact thoroughly tamed until its conquest by France in 1830.

Look a-head, look a-stern, look the weath-er in the lee,____ Blow high,____ blow low,____ And so____ sailed____ we. There's a loft-y ship to star-board and she's sail-ing fast and free, Sail-ing down a-long the coasts of High Bar-ba-ree.

Em      B7     Em
"Oh, are you a pirate or a man-o-war?" cried we.
    D  C  B7
Blow high, blow low, and so sailed we.
  Em   D   C    B7
"Oh no, I'm not a pirate but a man-o-war," cried he.
  Em        D Em
Sailing down along the coasts of High Barbaree.

Em      B7    Em
"We'll back up our topsail and heave our vessel to."
     D  C  B7
Blow high, blow low, and so sailed we.
  Em   D   C    B7
"But only in some harbor and along the side of you."
  Em        D Em
Sailing down along the coasts of High Barbaree.

Em      B7    Em
"Then back up your topsails and heave your vessel to."
     D  C  B7
Blow high, blow low, and so sailed we.
  Em   D   C    B7
"For we have got some letters to be carried home by you."
  Em        D Em
Sailing down along the coasts of High Barbaree.

Em      B7    Em
For broadside and broadside they fought all on the main.
     D  C  B7
Blow high, blow low, and so sailed we.
  Em   D   C    B7
Until at last the frigate shot the pirate's mast away.
  Em        D Em
Sailing down along the coasts of High Barbaree.

| Em | B7 | Em |
|---|---|---|

For quarter, for quarter, the saucy pirates cried.

| | D | C | B7 |
|---|---|---|---|

Blow high, blow low, and so sailed we.

| Em | D | C | B7 |
|---|---|---|---|

But the quarter that we showed them was to sink them in the tide.

| Em | | D Em |
|---|---|---|

Sailing down along the coasts of High Barbaree.

| Em | B7 | Em |
|---|---|---|

With cutlass and gun, oh, we fought for hours three.

| | D | C | B7 |
|---|---|---|---|

Blow high, blow low, and so sailed we.

| Em | D | C | B7 |
|---|---|---|---|

The ship it was their coffin, and their grave it was the sea.

| Em | | D Em |
|---|---|---|

Sailing down along the coasts of High Barbaree.

# Haul on the Bowline

This is a short-drag shanty used as a method of coordinating pulling, hauling and hoisting.

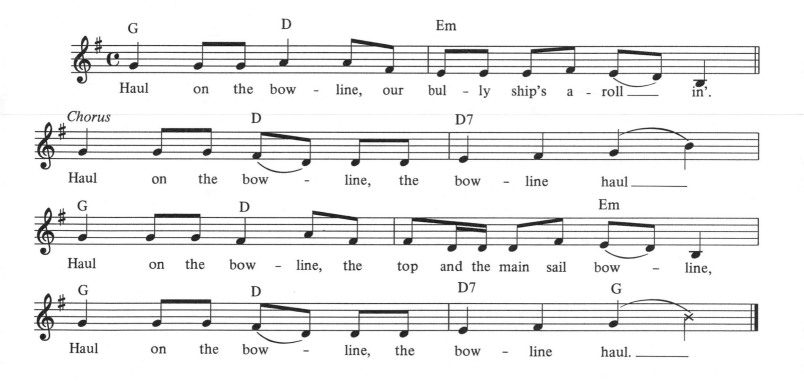

Haul on the bow-line, our bul-ly ship's a-roll—in'.

*Chorus*

Haul on the bow-line, the bow-line haul——

Haul on the bow-line, the top and the main sail bow-line,

Haul on the bow-line, the bow-line haul.——

| G | D | Em |
|---|---|---|

Haul on the bowline, Kitty is my darling, *Chorus*

| G | D | Em |
|---|---|---|

Haul on the bowline, the old man is **a-growlin'.** *Chorus*

| G | D | Em |
|---|---|---|

Haul on the bowline, Kitty lives at Liverpool, *Chorus*

| G | D | Em |
|---|---|---|

Haul on the bowline, it's a far cry to payday. *Chorus*

| G | D | Em |
|---|---|---|

Haul on the bowline, so early in the mornin'. *Chorus*

# Captain Kidd

William Kidd (*c.* 1645–1701) received a king's commission in 1696 to arrest and bring to trial all pirates. He sailed from Plymouth in May 1696 for New York, where he filled up his crew, and in 1697 reached Madagascar, the pirates' principal rendezvous. He made no effort whatsoever to hunt them down. On the contrary, he associated himself with a notorious pirate named Culliford. During 1698–1699 complaints reached the British government as to the character of his proceedings. He sailed again for America and buried some of his treasure on Gardiner's Island (off the east end of Long Island). He was arrested in Boston in July 1699 and was sent to England, where he was tried, convicted, and executed.

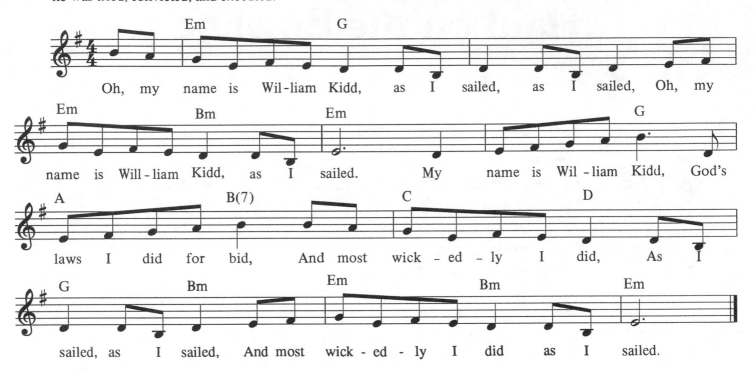

Oh, my name is Wil-liam Kidd, as I sailed, as I sailed, Oh, my name is Will-liam Kidd, as I sailed. My name is Wil-liam Kidd, God's laws I did for bid, And most wick-ed-ly I did, As I sailed, as I sailed, And most wick-ed-ly I did as I sailed.

    Em         G
Oh! my parents taught me well, as I sailed, as I sailed,
    Em         Bm    Em
Oh, my parents taught me well, as I sailed.
            G   A       B(7)
My parents taught me well, to shun the gates of hell,
    C       D     G    Bm
But against them I rebelled, as I sailed, as I sailed,
    Em     Bm    Em
But against them I rebelled, as I sailed.

    Em         G
I murdered William Moore, as I sailed, as I sailed,
    Em         Bm    Em
I murdered William Moore, as I sailed.
            G   A       B(7)
I murdered William Moore and left him in his gore,
    C       D     G    Bm
Not many leagues from shore, as I sailed, as I sailed,
    Em     Bm    Em
Not many leagues from shore, as I sailed.

    Em         G
And being cruel still, as I sailed, as I sailed,
    Em Bm    Em
And being cruel still, as I sailed,
            G   A       B(7)
And being cruel still, my gunner I did kill,
    C       D     G    Bm
And his precious blood did spill, as I sailed, as I sailed,
    Em     Bm    Em
And his precious blood did spill, as I sailed.

    Em         G
My mate was sick and died, as I sailed, as I sailed,
    Em         Bm    Em
My mate was sick and died, as I sailed.
            G   A       B(7)
My mate was sick and died, which me much terrified.
    C       D     G    Bm
He called me to his bedside, as I sailed, as I sailed,
    Em     Bm    Em
He called me to his bedside, as I sailed.

    Em         G
And unto me did say, "See me die, see me die,"
    Em         Bm    Em
And unto me did say, "See me die."
            G   A       B(7)
And unto me did say, "Take warning now by me,
    C       D     G    Bm
There comes a reckoning day, you must die, you must die,
    Em     Bm    Em
There comes a reckoning day, you must die."

    Em         G
I steered from sound to sound, as I sailed, as I sailed,
    Em         Bm    Em
I steered from sound to sound, as I sailed.
            G   A       B(7)
I steered from sound to sound, and many ships I found,
    C       D     G    Bm
And most of them I drowned, as I sailed, as I sailed,
    Em     Bm    Em
And most of them I drowned, as I sailed.

Em           G
I spied three ships from Spain, as I sailed, as I sailed,
Em            Bm     Em
I spied three ships from Spain, as I sailed.
                G      A      B(7)
I spied three ships from Spain, I fired on them amain
C         D     G     Bm
'Til most of them were slain, as I sailed, as I sailed,
Em          Bm     Em
'Til most of them were slain, as I sailed.

      Em         G
I'd ninety bars of gold, as I sailed, as I sailed,
Em          Bm     Em
I'd ninety bars of gold, as I sailed.
              G     A    B(7)
I'd ninety bars of gold, and dollars manifold,
C         D     G     Bm
With riches uncontrolled, as I sailed, as I sailed,
Em         Bm     Em
With riches uncontrolled, as I sailed.

          Em       G
Then fourteen ships I saw, as I sailed, as I sailed,
       Em        Bm     Em
Then fourteen ships I saw, as I sailed.
                G     A      B(7)
Then fourteen ships I saw, and brave men they were.
        C        D     G     Bm
Ah! they were too much for me, as I sailed, as I sailed,
          Em      Bm     Em
Ah! they were too much for me, as I sailed.

          Em       G
To Newgate I am cast, and must die, and must die,
       Em        Bm     Em
To Newgate I am cast, and must die.
              G     A      B(7)
To Newgate I am cast, with sad and heavy heart,
        C        D     G     Bm
To receive my just desert, I must die, I must die,
          Em      Bm     Em
To receive my just desert, I must die.

              Em       G
Take warning now by me, for I must die, I must die,
            Em      Bm     Em
Take warning now by me, for I must die.
              G     A      B(7)
Take warning now by me, and shun bad company,
        C        D     G     Bm
Lest you come to hell with me, for I must die, I must die,
          Em      Bm     Em
Lest you come to hell with me, for I must die.

# Johnny Todd

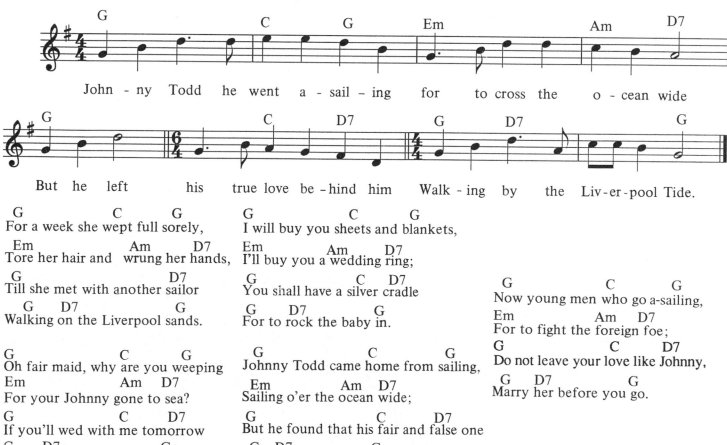

John - ny Todd he went a - sail - ing for to cross the o - cean wide
But he left his true love be - hind him Walk - ing by the Liv-er-pool Tide.

G         C     G
For a week she wept full sorely,
Em          Am    D7
Tore her hair and wrung her hands,
G               D7
Till she met with another sailor
  G   D7         G
Walking on the Liverpool sands.

G         C     G
Oh fair maid, why are you weeping
Em          Am    D7
For your Johnny gone to sea?
G         C    D7
If you'll wed with me tomorrow
G   D7         G
I will kind and constant be.

G         C     G
I will buy you sheets and blankets,
Em         Am    D7
I'll buy you a wedding ring;
G         C  D7
You shall have a silver cradle
G   D7      G
For to rock the baby in.

G         C     G
Johnny Todd came home from sailing,
Em         Am    D7
Sailing o'er the ocean wide;
G         C    D7
But he found that his fair and false one
G   D7      G
Was another sailor's bride.

G         C     G
Now young men who go a-sailing,
Em         Am    D7
For to fight the foreign foe;
G         C    D7
Do not leave your love like Johnny,
G   D7      G
Marry her before you go.

# The Golden Vanity

In hundreds of variations, this ballad has long been one of the most popular on both sides of the Atlantic. Francis J. Child traces the song back to a 17th century broadside in which Sir Walter Raleigh is named as the owner of the ship (there named *The Sweet Trinity*).

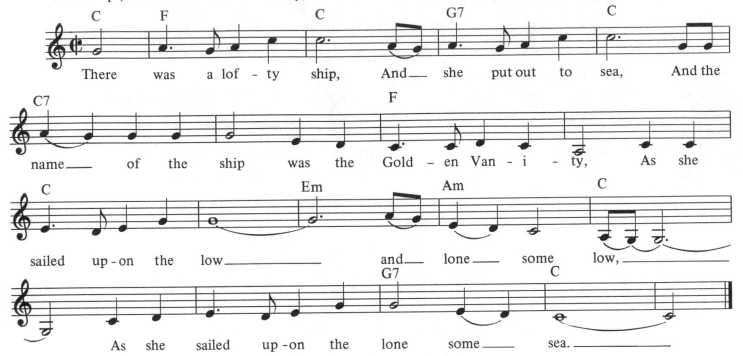

There was a lof - ty ship, And she put out to sea, And the
name of the ship was the Gold - en Van - i - ty, As she
sailed up - on the low and lone some low,
As she sailed up - on the lone some sea.

C    F        C   G7         C
She had not been out but two weeks or three,
      C7                         F
When she was overtaken by a Turkish Revelee,
      C              Em    Am      C
As she sailed upon the low and lonesome low,
                  G7         C
As she sailed upon the lonesome sea.

C    F  C     G7      C
Then up spake our little cabin boy,
          C7                              F
Saying, "What will you give me if I will them destroy,
      C              Em    Am      C
If I sink them in the low and lonesome low,
              G7         C
If I sink them in the lonesome sea?"

C        F           C     G7        C
"Oh, the man that them destroys," our captain then replied,
C7                                      F
"Five thousand pounds and my daughter for his bride,
      C              Em    Am      C
If he sinks them in the low and lonesome low,
                 G7         C
If he sinks them in the lonesome sea."

C        F          C     G7        C
Then the boy smote his breast and down jumped he,
        C7                           F
He swum 'til he came to the Turkish Revelee,
      C              Em    Am      C
As she sailed upon the low and lonesome low,
                  G7         C
As she sailed upon the lonesome sea.

C    F        C       G7        C
He had a little tool that was made for the use,
      C7                         F
He bored nine holes in her hull all at once,
      C              Em    Am      C
And he sunk her in the low and lonesome low,
                G7         C
He sunk her in the lonesome sea.

C    F          C       G7          C
He swum back to his ship and he beat upon the side,
         C7                              F
Cried, "Captain, pick me up for I'm wearied with the tide,
      C              Em    Am      C
I am sinking in the low and lonesome low,
                 G7         C
I am sinking in the lonesome sea."

```
       C   F        C     G7    C                      C   F        C     G7      C
"No! I will not pick you up," the captain replied,     "If it was not for the love that I bear for your men,
       C7                                    F              C7                  F
"I will shoot you, I will drown you, I will sink you in the tide.   I would do unto you as I did unto 'them.'
       C         Em    Am     C                             C        Em    Am      C
I will sink you in the low and lonesome low,           I would sink you in the low and lonesome low,
             G7        C                                           G7         C
I will sink you in the lonesome sea."                  I would sink you in the lonesome sea."
```

```
                   C   F        C     G7      C
         Then the boy bowed his head and down sunk he,
                   C7                    F
         Farewell, farewell to the Golden Vanity,
                   C        Em    Am      C
         As she sails upon the low and lonesome low,
                            G7        C
         As she sails upon the lonesome sea.
```

# Haul Away, Joe

"The shantyman with originality and a reputation to maintain tried not to repeat the same line twice. If his story came to an end before the job was over, he fell back on a series of lines describing the piece of work under way, drawn from a common stock used for 'piecing out' on such occasions." (Joanna Colcord, *Songs of American Sailormen*)

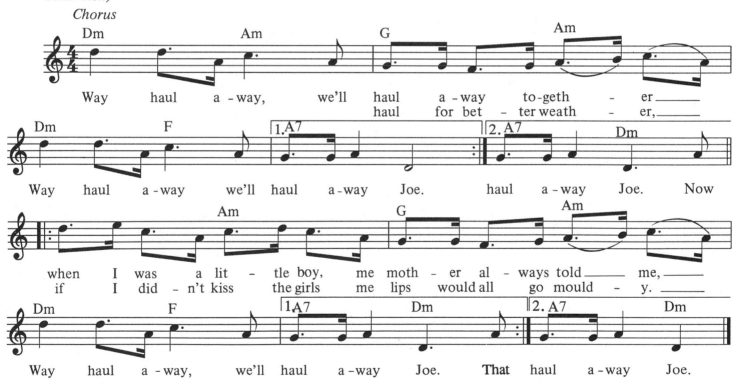

```
         Dm          Am          G           Am
King Louis was the king of France before the Revolution,
Dm       F       A7      Dm
Way haul away, we'll haul away, Joe.
                 Am          G           Am
But then he got his head cut off, which spoiled his constitution,
Dm       F       A7      Dm
Way haul away, we'll haul away, Joe. Chorus
```

```
         Dm          Am          G           Am
Once I had a German girl and she was fat and lazy,
Dm       F       A7      Dm
Way haul away, we'll haul away, Joe.
                 Am          G           Am
And then I had an Irish girl - she damn near drove me crazy,
Dm       F       A7      Dm
Way haul away, we'll haul away, Joe. Chorus
```

```
         Dm          Am          G           Am
Then I had a scolding wife, she wasn't very civil,
Dm       F       A7      Dm
Way haul away, we'll haul away, Joe.
```

```
         Dm          Am          G           Am
I clapped a plaster on her mouth and sent her to the divil,
Dm       F       A7      Dm
Way haul away, we'll haul away, Joe. Chorus
```

# Get Up, Jack

E        B7

Ships may come and ships may go, as long as the sea does

E        B7

roll, Each sail – or lad, like – wise his dad, he loves that flow – ing

E        A      E

bowl. A lass a – shore he does a – dore, one that is plump and

B7       E      B7    *Chorus*

round,— But when his mon – ey is gone, it's the same old song, 'Get

E

up, Jack! John, sit – down!" Come a – long, come a – long, my

A      E      B7

jol – ly brave tars, There's lots of grog in the jar,——— We'll

E      B7         E

plough the brin – y o – cean With those jol – ly rov – ing tars.

   E      B7       E
When Jack's ashore, he beats his way to some boarding house,
      B7          E
He's welcomed in with rum and gin, likewise with port and souse,
        A   E   B7
He'll spend and spend and never offend till he lies drunk on the ground,
     E    B7
But when his money is gone, it's the same old song. . . *Chorus*


     E    B7         E
Now when Jack is old and weather-beaten, too old to knock about,
      B7         E
In some grogshop they'll let him stop, till eight bells he's turned out.
      A     E    B7
Then he cries and he sighs right up to the skies: "Good Lord, I'm homeward bound,"
    E    B7
For when your money is gone, it's the same old song. . . *Chorus*

# The Fireship

As I walked out one ev-e-ning up-on my night's ca-reer, I spied a pret-ry fire-ship, and to her I did steer. I hoist-ed up my sig-a-nal, which she did quick-ly view,___ And when I had my bunt-ing up, she im-med-iate-ly hove to.___ She had a dark and a rov-ing eye,___ and her hair hung down in ring-e-lets,___ A nice girl, a de-cent girl, but one of the rak-ish kind.

G                                    D7
"Excuse me, sir," she said to me, "for being out so late.
G                                    D7
For if my parents knew of this, then sad would be my fate.
                        G      E7       Am
My father is a minister — a good and virtuous man,
       D7      G  C    A7       D7 C#ºD7
My mother is a Methodist — I do the best I ca-a-an." *Chorus*

                        G                      D7
I took her to a tav-er-in and treated her with wine.
                        G                      D7
Oh, little did I ever think that she was of the rakish kind.
                        G      E7       Am
I handled her, I dandled her — but much to my surprise,
       D7      G  C    A7       D7 C#º D7
She was only an old pirate ship rigged up in a disgui-i-ise. *Chorus*

                        G                      D7
So listen all you sailor men who sail upon the sea,
                        G                      D7
Beware of them there fireships — one was the ruin of me.
                        G      E7       Am
Beware of them, stay clear of them — they'll be the ruin of you;
       D7      G  C    A7       D7 C#º D7
'Twas there I had my mizzen sprung and my strong-box broken thru–u — u. *Chorus*

# Ten Thousand Miles Away

"At a time when the British statute-book bristled with capital felonies, when then the pickpocket or sheep-stealer was hanged out of hand, when Sir Samuel Romilly . . . declared that the laws of England were written in blood, another and less sanguinary penalty came into great favour. The deportation of criminals beyond the seas . . . the 'first fleet' of Australian annals reached Botany Bay in January 1788. . . ." (*Encyclopedia Britannica*, 1911 edition)

Sing ho! for a brave and a gal-lant ship, And a fair and fav-'ring
car-ry me o-ver the seas, my boys, To my true love far a-

breeze, With a bul-ly crew and a cap-tain too, To car-ry me o-ver the
way I'm tak-ing a trip on a

seas. To Gov-ern-ment ship, Ten thou-sand miles a-way.

*Chorus:* Then blow, ye winds, heigh-o! A-roving I will go.
       C         F

          C        G7
I'll stay no more on England's shore, to hear the music play.

     C           F
I'm off on the morning train to cross the raging main.

         C     F     C
I'm taking a trip on a Government ship ten thousand miles away.

   C               F
My true love she was handsome, my true love she was young,

        C          G7
Her eyes were blue as the violet's hue, and silvery was sound of her tongue;

   C              F
And silvery was the sound of her tongue, my boys, and, while I sing this lay,

         C    F   C
She's a-doing of the grand in a far-off land, ten thousand miles away!   *Chorus*

   C             F
Dark and dismal was the day when last I seen my Meg,

        C          G7
She'd a Goverment band around each hand, and another one round her leg;

   C              F
And another one round her leg, my boys, as the big ship left the bay,

        C    F    C
Adieu, said she, remember me, ten thousand miles away!   *Chorus*

   C             F
Oh! if I were a sailor, lad, or even a bombardier,

        C          G7
I'd hire a boat and go afloat, and straight to my true love steer;

   C              F
And straight to my true love steer, my boys, where the dancing dolphins play,

        C    F    C
And the whales and sharks kick up their larks, ten thousand miles away!   *Chorus*

```
         C                                                          F
The sun may shine through a London fog, or the river run bright and clear,
                        C                             G7
The ocean's brine be changed to wine, and I forget my beer,
        C                                              F
And I forget my beer, my boys, or the landlord's quarter day,
                             C              F          C
But never will I part from my own sweetheart ten thousand miles away.   *Chorus*
```

# What Shall We Do with the Drunken Sailor?

What shall we do with the drunk-en sail-or? What shall we do with the drunk-en sail-or? What shall we do with the drunk en sail-or? Ear-lye in the morn – ing.

*Chorus:*
**Dm**
Hooray, and up she rises,
**C**
Hooray, and up she rises,
**Dm**
Hooray, and up she rises,
**C**        **Dm**
Earlye in the morning.

**Dm**
Put him in a long boat till he's sober,
**C**
Put him in a long boat till he's sober,
**Dm**
Put him in a long boat till he's sober,
**C**        **Dm**
Earlye in the morning.    *Chorus*

**Dm**
Hang him by the leg in a running bowline,
**C**
Hang him by the leg in a running bowline,
**Dm**
Hang him by the leg in a running bowline,
**C**        **Dm**
Earlye in the morning.    *Chorus*

**Dm**
Put him in the scuppers with a hose pipe on him,
**C**
Put him in the scuppers with a hose pipe on him,
**Dm**
Put him in the scuppers with a hose pipe on him,
**C**        **Dm**
Earlye in the morning.    *Chorus*

**Dm**
Shave his belly with a rusty razor,
**C**
Shave his belly with a rusty razor,
**Dm**
Shave his belly with a rusty razor,
**C**        **Dm**
Earlye in the morning.    *Chorus*

**Dm**
That's what we'll do with the drunken sailor,
**C**
That's what we'll do with the drunken sailor,
**Dm**
That's what we'll do with the drunken sailor,
**C**        **Dm**
Earlye in the morning.    *Chorus*

# Blow the Man Down

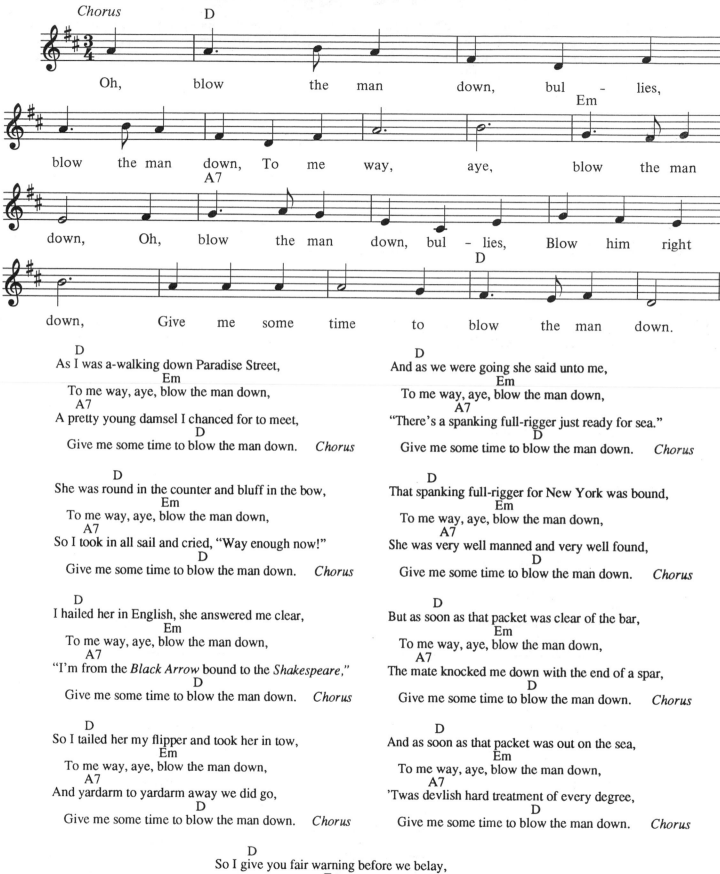

*Chorus*

Oh, blow the man down, bul - lies, blow the man down, To me way, aye, blow the man down, Oh, blow the man down, bul - lies, Blow him right down, Give me some time to blow the man down.

**D**
As I was a-walking down Paradise Street,
**Em**
To me way, aye, blow the man down,
**A7**
A pretty young damsel I chanced for to meet,
**D**
Give me some time to blow the man down.     *Chorus*

**D**
She was round in the counter and bluff in the bow,
**Em**
To me way, aye, blow the man down,
**A7**
So I took in all sail and cried, "Way enough now!"
**D**
Give me some time to blow the man down.     *Chorus*

**D**
I hailed her in English, she answered me clear,
**Em**
To me way, aye, blow the man down,
**A7**
"I'm from the *Black Arrow* bound to the *Shakespeare*,"
**D**
Give me some time to blow the man down.     *Chorus*

**D**
So I tailed her my flipper and took her in tow,
**Em**
To me way, aye, blow the man down,
**A7**
And yardarm to yardarm away we did go,
**D**
Give me some time to blow the man down.     *Chorus*

**D**
And as we were going she said unto me,
**Em**
To me way, aye, blow the man down,
**A7**
"There's a spanking full-rigger just ready for sea."
**D**
Give me some time to blow the man down.     *Chorus*

**D**
That spanking full-rigger for New York was bound,
**Em**
To me way, aye, blow the man down,
**A7**
She was very well manned and very well found,
**D**
Give me some time to blow the man down.     *Chorus*

**D**
But as soon as that packet was clear of the bar,
**Em**
To me way, aye, blow the man down,
**A7**
The mate knocked me down with the end of a spar,
**D**
Give me some time to blow the man down.     *Chorus*

**D**
And as soon as that packet was out on the sea,
**Em**
To me way, aye, blow the man down,
**A7**
'Twas devlish hard treatment of every degree,
**D**
Give me some time to blow the man down.     *Chorus*

**D**
So I give you fair warning before we belay,
**Em**
To me way, aye, blow the man down,
**A7**
Don't never take heed of what pretty girls say,
**D**
Give me some time to blow the man down.     *Chorus*

# Boney

While the British and French navies fought each other up and down the high seas for hundreds of years, the sailors of the warring fleets exchanged songs, verses and phrases. Thus, the perennial "oh, my boys" of the British chanty emerged on the other side of the Channel as, *"oh, mes boués."* This shanty about the rise and fall of Napoleon Bonaparte has its French counterpart as well:

> C'est Jean-François de Nantes,
> Oué, oué, oué.
> Gabier de la *Fringante*
> Oh, mes boués!
> Jean-François.

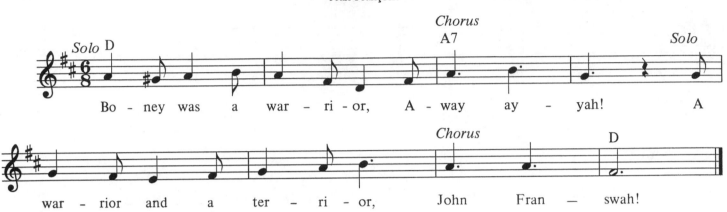

D
Boney beat the Prooshians,
A7
Away, ay-yah!
A7
Boney beat the Rooshians,
D
John Franswah!

D
Boney went to Moscow
A7
Away, ay-yah!
A7
Moscow was a-blazing,
D
John Franswah!

D
Boney went to Elbow,*
A7
Away, ay-yah!
A7
Boney he came back,
D
John Franswah!

D
Boney went to Waterloo,
A7
Away, ay-yah!
A7
There he got his overthrow,
D
John Franswah!

D
They took Boney off again,
A7
Away, ay-yah!
A7
'Board the *Billy Ruffian,***
D
John Franswah!

D
Boney he was sent away,
A7
Away, ay-yah!
A7
'Way to St. Helena,
D
John Franswah!

D
Boney broke his heart and died,
A7
Away, ay-yah!
A7
Boney broke his heart and died,
D
John Franswah!

*Elba
**H.M.S. Bellerophon, a ship on which Napoleon sailed.

# The Young Sailor Cut Down in His Prime

The sad tale of this young sailor wound up in Texas transformed into "The Streets of Laredo" — "the young cowboy who knew he done wrong."

He asked for a candle to light him to bed,  
Likewise a flannel to wrap 'round his head,  
For his poor head was aching, his poor heart was breaking,  
And he was a sailor cut down in his prime. *Chorus*

His poor old father, his good old mother  
Oft-times had told him about his past life.  
When along with those flash girls his money he squandered,  
And along with those flash girls he took his own life. *Chorus*

And now he is dead and he lies in his coffin,  
Six jolly sailors to carry him along,  
Six jolly maidens shall carry white roses,  
Not for to smell him as you pass him by. *Chorus*

On the top of the street you will see two girls standing,  
One to the other they whispered and said:  
"Here comes the young man whose money we squandered,  
Here comes the young sailor who's now cold and dead. *Chorus*

On the top of his headstone you'll see these words written,  
All you young men take a warning by me,  
And never go courting with the girls in the city,  
Flash girls of the city were the ruin of me. *Chorus*

# Little Sally Racket

*Solo* D
Lit – tle Sal – ly Rack – et, *Chorus* G D Haul – 'em a – way,

*Solo* *Chorus* G D A
Shipped a board a pack – et, Haul – 'em a – way, And she nev – er did re – gret it,

*Chorus* G D G D
Haul – 'em a – way, With a haul – ey hi o, Haul – 'em a – way.

D
Little Kitty Carson . . .

Slept with a parson . . .

A
Now she's got a little barson. . .

D
Little Nancy Riddle. . .

Broke her brand new fiddle . . .

A
Got a hole right up the middle. .

D
Little Nancy Tucket. . .

Washes in a bucket. . .

A
She's a whore, but doesn't look it. . .

D
Little Polly Skinner. . .

Says she's a beginner. . .

A
She prefers it to her dinner. . .

D
Little Nancy Taylor. . .

Would never touch a sailor . . .

A
'Til she was harpooned by a whaler. . .

# A-Roving

E B7 E B7 E
In Am – ster-dam there lives a maid Mark well what I do say, In

A E F#m F#7 E B7
Am – ster-dam there lives a maid, And she is mis – tress of her trade. I'll

E A E B7 E
go no more a rov – ing with you, fair maid.

*Chorus* A E F#m F#7 E B7
A – rov – ing, a – rov – ing, since rov-ing's been my___ ru – i – in, I'll

E A E B7 E
go no more a – rov – ing with you, fair maid,

    E      B7     E      B7
Her eyes are like two stars so bright,
         E
Mark well what I do say!
   A         E
Her eyes are like two stars so bright,
  F#m F#7   E    B7
Her face is fair, her step is light,
     E        A     E  B7 E
And I'll go no more a-roving with you, fair maid! *Chorus*

    E      B7     E      B7
Her cheeks are like the rosebuds red,
         E
Mark well what I do say!
   A         E
Her cheeks are like the rosebuds red;
    F#m  F#7 E     B7
There's a wealth of hair upon her head,
    E        A     E  B7 E
And I'll go no more a-roving with you, fair maid! *Chorus*

    E      B7     E      B7
I took the maiden for a walk,
         E
Mark well what I do say!
   A         E
I took the maiden for a walk
  F#m     F#7 B7
And sweet and loving was our talk,
    E        A     E  B7 E
And I'll go no more a-roving with you, fair maid! *Chorus*

    E      B7     E      B7
I took the maiden on my knee,
         E
Mark well what I do say!
   A         E
I took the maiden on my knee,
  F#m     F#7     E    B7
She said, "Young man, you're rather free."
    E        A     E  B7  E
And I'll go no more a-roving with you, fair maid! *Chorus*

    E      B7     E      B7
I put my arm around her waist,
         E
Mark well what I do say!
   A         E
I put my arm around her waist,
  F#m     F#7     E    B7
She said, "Young man, you're in great haste."
    E        A     E  B7, E
And I'll go no more a-roving with you, fair maid! *Chorus*

    E      B7     E      B7
I love this fair maid my life,
         E
Mark well what I do say.
   A         E
I love this fair maid as my life,
  F#m    F#7   E    B7
And soon she'll be my little wife;
    E        A     E  B7 E
I'll go no more a-roving with you, fair maid! *Chorus*

        E      B7     E      B7
And if you'd know this maiden's name,
             E
Mark well what I do say.
       A           E
And if you'd know this maiden's name,
    F#m   F#7    E    B7
Why soon like mine, 'twill be the same;
      E        A     E  B7 E
I'll go no more a-roving with you, fair maid. *Chorus*

# The Leaving of Liverpool

| | C | | | F | C |
|---|---|---|---|---|---|
| I'm off to California | | | | | |
| | | F | C | G | |
| By the way of the stormy Cape Horn, | | | | | |
| | C | | F | C | |
| And I will send to you a letter, love, | | | | | |
| | | G7 | C | | |
| When I am homeward bound. *Chorus* | | | | | |

I've shipped on a Yankee clipper ship,
            F  C  G
*Davy Crockett* is her name,
    C           F  C
And Burgess is the captain of her,
                G7  C
And they say she's a floating shame. *Chorus*

---

**C**          **F**  **C**
Farewell to Lower Frederick Street,
           F  C  G
Anson Terrace and Park Lane.
  C            F  C
Farewell, it will be some long time
    G7     C
Before I see you again.     *Chorus*

         C         F  C
The tug is waiting at the pierhead
            F  C  G
To take us from the shore,
    C            F  C
Our sails are loose and our anchor secure,
               G7     C
So I'll bid you good-bye once more. *Chorus*

---

        C         F  C
I'm bound away to leave you,
              F  C  G
Good-bye, my love, good-bye.
        C         F  C
There ain't but one thing that grieves me,
        G7  C
That's leaving you behind. *Chorus*

# Benbow, the Brother Tar

John Benbow (1653–1702) served as vice-admiral under William III. In 1701 he was sent to the West Indies as commander-in-chief. On August 19, 1702, when cruising with a squadron of seven ships, he sighted and chased four French vessels near Santa Marta. What then transpired has been described as the most disgraceful episode in English naval history. We get this description of the encounter from a contemporary diary:

News of Vice-Admiral Benbow's conflict with the French fleet in the West Indies, in which he gallantly behaved himself, was wounded, and would have had extraordinary success, had not four of his men-of-war stood spectators without coming to his assistance; for this two of their commanders were tried by a council of war and executed; a third was condemned to perpetual imprisonment, loss of pay, and incapacity to serve in future. The fourth died.

Come all you sail-ors bold, lend an ear, lend an ear. Come all you sail-ors bold, lend an ear. It's of our Ad-miral's fame, Brave Ben-bow call'd by name. How he fought on the main you shall hear, you shall hear. How hear.

Am E Am
Brave Benbow he set sail
G Dm
For to fight, for to fight.
E7 Am E Am
Brave Benbow he set sail for to fight,
C Dm
Brave Benbow he set sail,
Am Dm E E7
With a fine and pleasant gale,
Am F Dm6 E7 Am
But his Captains they turned tail ⎤
E7 Am E Am (E7 1st time) ⎥ 2
In a fright, in a fright. ⎦

Am E Am
Says Kirby unto Wade,
G Dm
"I will run, I will run."
E7 Am E Am
Says Kirby unto Wade, "I will run.
C Dm
I value not disgrace,
Am Dm E E7
Nor the losing of my place,
Am F Dm6 E7 Am
But the French I will not face ⎤
E7 Am E Am (E7) ⎥ 2
With a gun, with a gun." ⎦

Am E Am
'Twas the *Ruby* and *Noah's Ark*
G Dm
Fought the French, fought the French.
E7 Am E Am
'Twas the *Ruby* and *Noah's Ark* fought the French.
C Dm
And there was ten in all,
Am Dm E E7
They fought them ball for ball.
Am F Dm6 E7 Am
The smoke it cast a pall, ⎤
E7 Am E Am (E7) ⎥ 2
And a stench, and a stench. ⎦

Am E Am
It was our Admiral's lot,
G Dm
With chain shot, with chain shot,
E7 Am E Am
It was our Admiral's lot, with chain shot.
C Dm
Our Admiral lost his legs,
Am Dm E E7
And to his men he begs,
Am F Dm6 E7 Am
"Fight on, my boys," he says, ⎤
E7 Am E Am (E7) ⎥ 2
"'Tis my lot, 'tis my lot." ⎦

Am E Am
While the surgeon dressed his wounds,
G Dm
Thus he said, thus he said,
E7 Am E Am
While the surgeon dressed his wounds, thus he said.
C Dm
"Let my cradle now in haste
Am Dm E E7
On the quarter-deck be placed,
Am F Dm6 E7 Am
That my enemies I may face ⎤
E7 Am E Am (E7) ⎥ 2
'Til I'm dead, 'til I'm dead. ⎦

Am E Am
And there bold Benbow lay
G Dm
In great pain, in great pain.
E7 Am E Am
And there bold Benbow lay, in great pain.
C Dm
"Let us tack about once more,
Am Dm E E7
We'll drive them to their own shore.
Am F Dm6 E7 Am
I value not half a score ⎤
E7 Am E Am (E7) ⎥ 2
We shall gain, we shall gain." ⎦

# The Bold Fisherman

Humphrey Bogart and Katherine Hepburn sang this song in the movie, *The African Queen.*

There was a bold fish – er-man who sailed out from Pim - be-co, To slew the wild cod fish and the bold mack - er - el. When he ar-rived off Pim - be-co, the storm – y winds did wild – ly blow. His lit – tle boat went wib - ble, wob-ble, And o - ver board sprang he. "Twink - i doo - dle dum, twink - i doo - dle dum," Twas the high – ly in - ter-est – ing song he sung. "Twink - i doo - dle dum, twink i doo - dle dum," sang the bold fish - er - man.

| D | | A7 | D |
|---|---|---|---|
He wriggled and he scriggled in the water so briny-o,

| | A7 | D | |
He yellowed and bellowed for help, but in vain.

| G | | D | |
Then downward he did gently glide

| A7 | | D | |
To the bottom of the silvery tide,

| G | | D | |
But previously to this he cried,

| A7 | D | |
"Fare thee well, Mar - i - jane!" *Chorus*

| D | | A7 | D |
His ghost walked at midnight to the bedside of Mar - i - jane.

| | A7 | D | |
He told her how dead he was - said she, "I'll go mad."

| G | | D | |
"Since my lovey is so dead." said she,

| A7 | | D | |
"All joy on earth has fled for me.

| G | | D | |
I never more will happy be."

| A7 | D | |
And she went staring mad. *Chorus*

94

# The Cruel War

This is the army equivalent of "The Handsome Cabin Boy."

The cruel war is rag – ing and John – ny has to

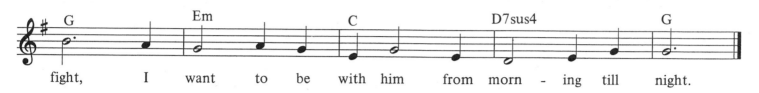

fight, I want to be with him from morn – ing till night.

G     Em     Am     G
I'll go to your captain, get down upon my knees,
    Em     C     D7/4     G
The thousand gold guineas I'd give for your release.

G     Em     Am     G
Your cheeks are too rosy, it grieves my heart so,
    Em     C     D7/4     G
Won't you let me go with you? Oh, no, my love, no.

G     Em     Am     G
Ten thousand gold guineas, it grieves my heart so;
    Em     C     D7/4     G
Won't you let me go with you? Oh, no, my love, no.

G     Em     Am     G
Johnny, oh Johnny, I think you are unkind.
    Em     C     D7/4     G
I love you far better than all other mankind.

G     Em     Am     G
Tomorrow is Sunday and Monday is the day
    Em     C     D7/4     G
Your captain calls for you, and you must obey.

G     Em     Am     G
I love you far better than tongue can express,
    Em     C     D7/4     G
Won't you let me go with you? Oh, yes, my love, yes.

G     Em     Am     G
Your captain calls for you, it grieves my heart so,
    Em     C     D7/4     G
Won't you let me go with you? Oh, no, my love, no.

G     Em     Am     G
I'll pull back my hair, men's clothes I'll put on,
    Em     C     D7/4     G
I'll pass for your comrade as we march along.

G     Em     Am     G
Your waist is too slender, your fingers are too small,
    Em     C     D7/4     G
Your cheeks are too rosy to face the cannonball.

G     Em     Am     G
I'll pass for your comrade and none will ever guess,
    Em     C     D7/4     G
Won't you let me go with you? - Yes, my love, yes.

D7sus4 (D7/4)

# High Germany

Another "May I come along too" ballad. This one dates from the Seven Years' War (1756–1763), in which a coalition of Austria, France, Russia, Sweden, and Saxony was formed to do battle with Prussia, with the object of destroying the power of Frederick the Great. Prussia was joined by England; and, as usual, a maritime and colonial war broke out between England and France. This war laid the foundations for the British Empire.

O Pol - ly dear, O Pol - ly, the rout has now be - gun, And we must march a - way at the beat - ing of the drum. Go dress your - self all in your best and come a - long with me, I'll take you to the cru - el wars in High Ger - ma - ny.

       Dm  C  Dm    F     Gm        Dm
I'll buy you a horse, my love, and on it you shall ride,
            F   C7  F   Bb   F   C7    F  C7
And all of my delight shall be riding by your side;
             F   Gm  F  Bb      Am      Bb     C
We'll call at every ale house, and drink when we are dry,
Bb   F   C7     Dm    Am      G         Dm
So quickly on the road, my love, we'll marry by and by.

      Dm   C  DmF    Gm        Dm
O Harry, dear Harry, you mind what I do say,
          F      C7    F Bb  F    C7     F  C7
My feet they are so tender I cannot march away,
          F      Gm  F Bb     Am   Bb      C
And besides, my dearest Harry, though I'm in love with thee,
Bb  F    C7    Dm  Am      G        Dm
I am not fit for cruel wars in High Germany.

      Dm   C     Dm  F    Gm        Dm
O cursed were the cruel wars that ever they should rise,
          F   C7    F Bb      F    C7     F  C7
And out of merry England press many a lad likewise!
          F      Gm  F Bb    Dm     Bb      C
They pressed young Harry from me, likewise my brothers three,
Bb  F    C7    Dm  Am      G        Dm
And sent them to the cruel wars in High Germany.

# An Invitation to North America

From an undated 18th-century London broadside.

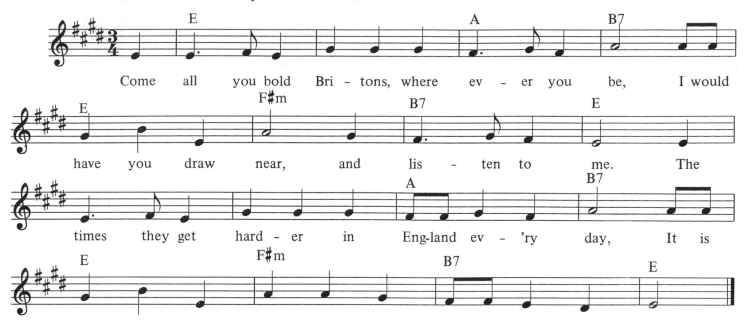

Come all you bold Bri - tons, where ev - er you be, I would
have you draw near, and lis - ten to me. The
times they get hard - er in Eng-land ev - 'ry day, It is
much bet - ter liv - ing in North A - me - ri - cay.

E  A  B7
There is many a family of late that has gone
E F#m B7 E
Away to New York, father, mother and son;
 A B7
Let us likewise follow and make no delay,
E F#m B7 E
For 'tis much cheaper living in North Americay.

E  A B7
The farmers in England sell their corn so dear,
E F#m B7 E
They do what they can to starve the poor here.
 A B7
They send it to France, which sure is not right,
E F#m B7 E
To feed other nations that against us do fight,
E  A B7
Why do we stay here for to be their slaves,
E F#m B7 E
When in Nova Scotia we can do as we please;
 A B7
For who'd work in England for ten pence a day,
E F#m B7 E
When we can get four shillings in North Americay.

E  A B7
There's many a farmer you very well know,
E F#m B7 E
That went to New York but a few years ago,
 A B7
Have bought land and houses; who now would here stay,
E F#m B7 E
But go and make fortunes in North Americay.

E  B7
The landlords in England do raise the lands high,
E F#m B7 E
It forces some farmers abroad for to fly;
 A B7
If times grow no better, I'll venture to say,
E F#m B7 E
Poor men had better go to North Americay.

E  A B7
Observe then, good people, what to you I've told,
E F#m B7 E
What a plague is in England by short weight of gold.
 A B7
With bad silver and halfpence, believe what I say,
E F#m B7 E
There's nothing of this in North Americay.

E  A B7
The priests in England come into the field,
E F#m B7 E
They tithe as they please, you dare not but yield;
 A B7
This is a great hardship, you believe, I dare say.
E F#m B7 E
But we'll have no taxes in North Americay.

E  A B7
Manufactures in England are grown very bad,
E F#m B7 E
For weavers and combers no work's to be had.
 A B7
But let's go abroad, I dare venture to say,
E F#m B7 E
They'll find us employment in North Americay.

E  A B7
So here's health to George our gracious king,
E F#m B7 E
I hope none will take amiss the song that I sing;
 A B7
Then lads and lasses now come away,
E F#m B7 E
And ship yourselves to North Americay.

# The British Grenadiers

John Evelyn (1620–1706) notes in his diary that on June 29, 1678, he saw at Hounslow "a new sort of soldiers called granadiers, who were dexterous in flinging hand-granades." This French practice was quickly copied by the English, and eventually each English battalion had a grenadier company.

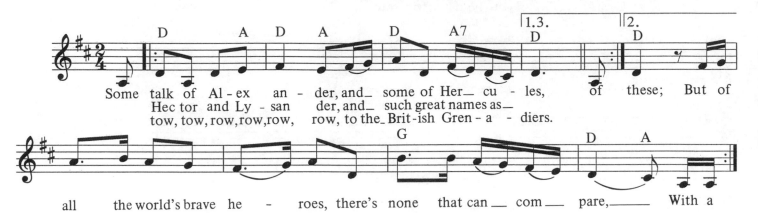

Some talk of Al - ex  an — der, and_ some of Her_ cu - les,  of  these;  But of
Hec tor and Ly - san  der, and_ such great names as_
tow, tow, row, row, row,  row, to the_ Brit-ish Gren - a - diers.

all  the world's brave he — roes, there's none  that can __ com __ pare, _____  With a

 

    D     A  D A   D      A7 D
Whene'er we are commanded to storm the palisades,
          A  DA   D      A7  D
Our leaders march with fuses and we with hand grenades.
                       D          D A
We throw them from the glacis about the enemy's ears.
    D       A  D A      D     A7 D
Sing tow, row, row, row, row, row, the British Grenadiers.

    D       A DA   D     A7   D
And when the siege is over, we to the town repair,
          A  DA      D     A7 D
The townsmen cry, "Hurrah, boys, here comes a Grenadier;
                        G         D A
Here come the Grenadiers, my boys, who know no doubts or fears."
        D          A D A      D  A7  D
With a tow, row, row, row, row, row, it's the British Grenadiers.

      D       A D A    D    A7     D
Then let us fill a bumper and drink a health to those
          A  D A     D      A7   D
Who carry caps and pouches, and wear the louped clothes,
                          G        D A
May they and their commanders live happy all their years,
        D         A  D A      D     A7 D
With a tow, row, row, row, row, row, for the British Grenadiers.

# How Happy the Soldier

Sung by British soldiers during the American Revolutionary War.

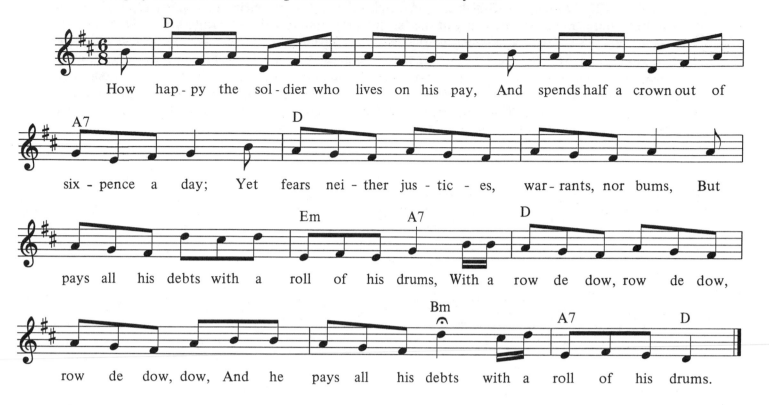

How hap-py the sol-dier who lives on his pay, And spends half a crown out of six-pence a day; Yet fears nei-ther jus-tic-es, war-rants, nor bums, But pays all his debts with a roll of his drums, With a row de dow, row de dow, row de dow, dow, And he pays all his debts with a roll of his drums.

D
He cares not a marvedy how the world goes,
A7
His King finds his quarters and money and clothes;
D
He laughts at all sorrow whenever it comes,
      Em      A7
And rattles away with the roll of his drums.
          D
With  row de dow, row de dow, row de dow, dow
    Bm      A7      D
And rattles away with the roll of his drums.

D
The drum is his glory, his joy and delight,
             A7
It leads him to pleasure as well as to fight;
D
No girl, when she hears it, though ever so glum,
             Em     A7
But packs up her tatters and follows the drum.
          D
With row de dow, row de dow, row de dow, dow,
      Bm     A7     D
She packs up her tatters and follows the drum.

# Brave Wolfe

James Wolfe (1727–1759) led the British army in the victorious attack on Quebec on September 13, 1759. This decisive battle in the French and Indian War was but an aspect of the previously mentioned Seven Years' War ("High Germany"). Wolfe had become engaged just before his departure from England (hence the line "They stole my love away. . . ."). Mortally wounded, he lay semi-conscious on the field of battle when someone near him exclaimed, "They run! See how they run!" "Who run?," Wolfe asked weakly, rousing from his swoon. "The enemy," was the answer, "they give way everywhere." Wolfe rallied for a moment, gave a last order for cutting off the retreat, and murmuring, "Now God be praised, I will die in peace," breathed his last. His opponent, French General Montcalm, survived him only a few hours.

| | | | |
|---|---|---|---|
| Em | B7 | | Em |
| Then away went this brave youth and embarked on the ocean, | | | |
| | B7 | Em | |
| To free Amerikay was his intention. | | | |
| Am | B7 | D7 | G |
| He landed in Quebec with all his party, | | | |
| Em | B7 | | Em |
| The city to attack, being brave and hearty. | | | |

Em       B7       Em
He drew his army up in lines so pretty,
      B7       Em
On the plains of Abraham, back of the city.
      Am       B7       D7       G
At a distance from the town where the French would meet him,
      Em       B7       Em
In double numbers there resolved to beat him.

Em       B7       Em
Montcalm and this brave youth together walked,
      B7       Em
Between two armies they, like brothers, talked.
      Am       B7       D7   G
'Til each one took his post and did retire,
      Em       B7       Em
It was then these numerous hosts commenced their fire.

Em       B7       Em
The drums did loudly beat, colours were flying,
      B7       Em
The purple gore did stream and men lay dying;
      Am       B7       D7       G
When shot from off his horse fell this brave hero,
      Em       B7       Em
And we lament his loss in weeds of sorrow.

Em       B7       Em
The French began to break their ranks and flying,
      B7       Em
Brave Wolfe then seemed to wake as he lay dying,
      Am       B7       D7       G
He lifted up his head while guns did rattle,
      Em       B7       Em
And to his army said, "How goes the battle?"

Em       B7       Em
His aide-de-camp replied, "'Tis in our favor.
      B7       Em
Quebec with all her pride, we soon shall have her;
      Am       B7       D7       G
She'll fall into our hands with all her treasure."
      Em       B7       Em
"Oh, then," replied brave Wolfe, "I die with pleasure."

# Why, Soldiers, Why?

General Wolfe is said to have ordered this song sung the night before the battle of Quebec (see "Brave Wolfe"). It dates from at least 1729, and has also been called "How Stands the Glass Around?" and "The Duke of Berwick's March." James Fitzjames, Duke of Berwick (1670–1734), was an extraordinary figure in both English and French military history. He was the son of James, Duke of York, afterwards James II, and Arabella Churchill, sister of the great Duke of Marlborough. After serving with distinction in various European campaigns with the British army, he took service with the French, eventually attaining the rank of marshall. As commander of the Franco-Spanish armies he won a decisive victory at Almanza (April 25, 1707). The victory established Philip V on the throne of Spain. It was a victory won by an Englishman, Berwick, at the head of a French army over a Frenchman, Ruvigny, Earl of Galway, at the head of an English army. Berwick was killed at the siege of Philipsburg on June 12, 1734. He amply deserves "his" march.

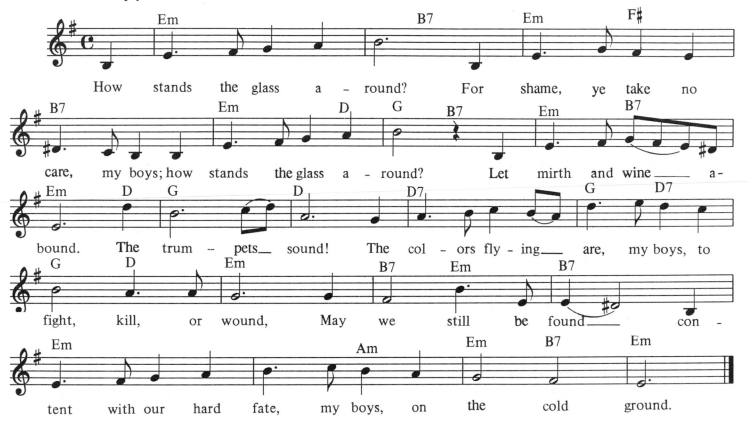

How stands the glass a - round? For shame, ye take no care, my boys; how stands the glass a - round? Let mirth and wine a-bound. The trum - pets sound! The col - ors fly - ing are, my boys, to fight, kill, or wound, May we still be found con - tent with our hard fate, my boys, on the cold ground.

Em    B7 Em F♯ B7
Why, soldiers, why should we be melancholy, boys?

Em  D  G B7  Em  B7 Em
Why, soldiers, why? Whose bus' ness 'tis to die.

 D   G   D  D7     G  D7
What? Sighing? Fie! Drink on, drown fear, be jolly, boys;

    G D Em  B7 Em  B7
'Tis he, you or I cold, hot, wet or dry,

      Em      Am    Em B7 Em
We're always bound to follow, boys, and scorn to fly.


     Em    B7 Em    F♯  B7
'Tis but in vain (I mean not to upbraid you, boys),

      EmD G B7 Em  B7    Em
'Tis but in vain for soldiers to complain.

     D   G   D    D7     G    D7
Should next campaign send us to Him that made you, boys,

      G  D Em     B7 Em B7
We're free from pain - but should we remain,

      Em        Am  Em B7 Em
A bottle and a kind landlady cure all again.

# To the Commons

This song, published in the *Middlesex Journal* in 1776, reflects British opposition at home to the "colonial war" in far-off America. The composer, who prudently identified himself only as "M," prefaced his song by saying, "Heaven help us if they will not take good advice, or stop for reflection, for they are speedily leading us to the devil."

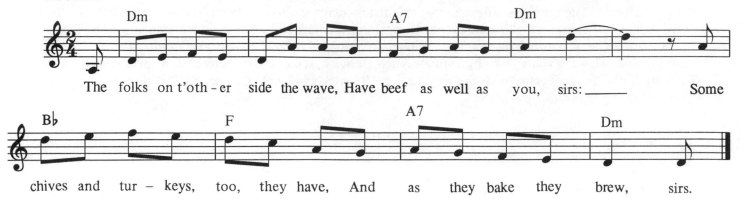

The folks on t'oth-er side the wave, Have beef as well as you, sirs:_____ Some chives and tur-keys, too, they have, And as they bake they brew, sirs.

Dm
What though your cannon raze their towns
 A7           Dm
And tumble down their houses,
 Bb              F
They'll fight like devils, blood and bones,
 A7           Dm
For children and for spouses.

Dm
Another truth - nay, 'tis no boast,
 A7           Dm
Nor yet the lie o' the day, sirs,
 Bb              F
The saints on Massachusetts coast
 A7           Dm
Gain if they run away, sirs.

Dm
For further than your bullets fly,
 A7           Dm
A common man may run, sirs,
 Bb              F
And wheat will grow beneath the sky
 A7           Dm
Where cannot reach a gun, sirs.

Dm
Then what are ships and swords and guns,
 A7           Dm
And men of bloody mind, sirs,
 Bb              F
While, Parthian-like, who conquers runs,
 A7           Dm
Who loses - stays behind, sirs.

Dm
Recall your ships, your troops recall,
 A7           Dm
Let friends each other nourish,
 Bb              F
So shall old England rule the ball
 A7                    Dm
And George and freedom flourish.

# The Dying British Sergeant

This song from the period of the American Revolutionary War is sometimes called "General Gage," after Thomas Gage (1721–1787), British general and colonial governor of Massachusetts up to the battle of Bunker Hill (June 15, 1775).

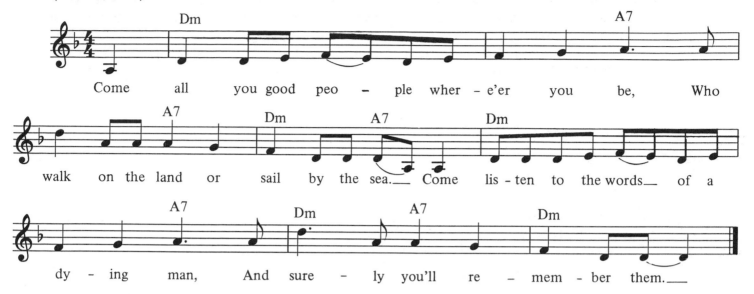

Come all you good peo — ple wher – e'er you be, Who walk on the land or sail by the sea. Come lis – ten to the words of a dy – ing man, And sure – ly you'll re — mem – ber them.

1. 'Twas in December, the sixteenth day,
That we set sail for Amerikay,
Our drums and trumpets loud did sound,
And unto Boston we were bound.

2. And when to Boston we did come,
We thought by the aid of our British guns,
To make these Yankees own our king,
And daily tribute to him bring.

3. But to our sorrow and surprise,
We saw them, like grasshoppers, rise,
They fought like heroes in much rage,
Which surely frightened General Gage.

4. Like lions roaring for their prey,
They feared no danger nor dismay;
True British blood runs through their veins,
And them, with courage, it sustains.

5. We saw those bold Columbia sons
Spread death and slaughter from their guns.
Freedom or death! was all their cry,
They did not seem to fear to die.

6. We sailed to York, sailed the Sound,
And many a traitor there we found,
Who told us we could win the day –
There was no danger, they did say.

7. They told us 'twas a garden place,
And that our armies could, with ease,
Pull down their towns, lay waste their lands,
In spite of all rebel bands.

8. A garden place it was indeed,
And in it grew many a bitter weed,
Which did pull down our highest hopes
And sorely wound the British troops.

9. 'Tis now September, the seventeenth day,
I wish I'd ne'er come to Americay.
Full fifteen hundred have been slain,
Bold British heroes every one.

10. Now I've received my deathly wound,
I bid farewell to England's ground;
My wife and children will mourn for me,
Whilst I lie cold in Amerikee.

11. Fight on, America's noble sons,
Fear not Britannia's thundering guns.
Maintain your rights from year to year,
God's on your side, you need not fear.

# Yankee Doodle's Expedition to Rhode Island

Published in Rivington's *Royalist Gazette* in New York on October 3, 1778, this loyalist barb recounts the failure of a combined American-French assault on the British garrison under the command of General Robert Pigot at Newport, Rhode Island, the previous August. A force of 10,000 rebel troops under the command of General John Sullivan, supported by a French fleet commanded by Count D'Estaing, failed to dislodge the British garrison, which numbered only 3,000. (Monsieur Gérard was Conrad Alexandre Gérard, the first French ambassador to the United States.)

From Lou - is, Mon -sieur Gér - ard came, to Con -gress in this town, sir. They bowed to him, and he to them, And then they all sat down, sir. "Be-gar," said Mon-sieur,"one grand *coup* You shall *bien-tôt* be-hold, sir," This was be-lieved as gos - pel true, And Jon _ a - than felt bold, sir.

G           D7
So Yankee Doodle did forget
G           D7
The sound of British drums, sir,
G           C
How oft it made him quake and sweat
  D7       G
In spite of Yankee rum, sir.
C
He took his wallet on his back,
  G
His rifle on his shoulder,
  C
And vowed Rhode Island to attack
  G    D7    G
Before he was much older.

     G            D7
In dread array, their tattered crew
     G            D7
Advanced with colours spread, sir,
     G            C
Their fifes played Yankee-doodle-doo,
   D7       G
King Hancock at their head, sir.
     C
What numbers bravely crossed the seas,
    G
I cannot well determine,
    C
A swarm of rebels and of fleas,
    G    D7   G
And every other vermin.

     G            D7
Their mighty hearts might shrink, they thought,
     G            D7
For all flesh only grass is,
     G            C
A piteous store they therefore brought
    D7        G
Of whiskey and molasses.
     C
They swore they'd make bold Pigot squeak,
    G
So did their good ally, sir,
    C
And take him pris'ner in a week,
    G   D7   G
But that was all my eye, sir.

     G            D7
As Jonathan so much desired
     G            D7
To shine in martial story,
     G            C
D'Estaing with *politesse* retired,
    D7        G
To leave him all the glory.
     C
He left him what was better yet,
    G
At least it was more use, sir,
    C
He left him for a quick retreat,
    G   D7   G
A very good excuse, sir.

                     G            D7
To stay unless he ruled the sea,
                     G            D7
He thought would not be right, sir.
                     G      C
And Continental troops, said he,
                  D7        G
On islands should not fight, sir.
                  C
Another cause with these combined,
                  G
To throw him in the dumps, sir,
                  C
For Clinton's name alarmed his mind
                  G    D7   G
And made him stir his stumps, sir.

# The Congress

In 1776, the Philadelphia publication *Towne's Evening Post* ran this lampoon directed against the Continental Congress.

When Jove resolved to send a curse,
And all the woes of life rehearse,
Not plague, not famine, but much worse;
  He cursed us with a Congress.
Then peace forsook this hapless shore,
Then cannons blazed with horrid roar;
We hear of blood, death, wounds and gore,
  The offspring of the Congress.

Good Lord! disperse this venal tribe,
Their doctrine let no fools imbibe,
Let Balaam no more asses ride,
  Nor burdens bear to Congress.
Old Catiline, and Cromwell too,
Jack Cade and his seditious crew,
Hail brother rebel at first view,
  And hope to meet the Congress.

There's Washington and all his men—
Where Howe had one, the goose had ten—
Marches up the hill and down again,
  And sent returns to Congress.
Prepare, prepare, my friends, prepare
For scenes of blood, the field of war;
To royal standard we'll repair,
  And curse the haughty Congress.

With freemen's rights they wanton play,
At their command, we fast and pray,
With worthless paper, they us pay,
  A fine device of Congress.
Time-serving priests to zealots preach,
Who king and parliament impeach,
Seditious lessons us to teach
  At the command of Congress.

The world's amazed to see the pest
The tranquil land with wars infest,
Britannia puts them to the test,
  And tries the strength of Congress.
Clinton, Burgoyne and gallant Howe
Will soon reward our conduct true,
And to each traitor give his due,
  Perdition waits the Congress.

*Sung to measures 9–16*
Huzza! huzza! we thrice huzza!
Return peace, harmony and law!
Restore such times as once we saw,
  And bid adieu to Congress.

# The Plains of Waterloo

"A Horbury correspondent sends me the . . . setting of 'The Plains of Waterloo,' as learned by his grandfather and himself from Waterloo men; he informing me that it was the tune preferred and mostly sung by the Waterloo heroes." (Frank Kidson, *Supplement to Old English Popular Music,* 1893)

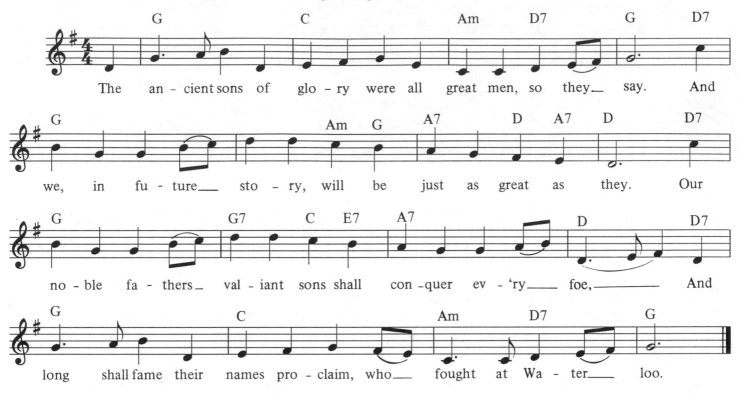

The an-cient sons of glo-ry were all great men, so they say. And
we, in fu-ture sto-ry, will be just as great as they. Our
no-ble fa-thers val-iant sons shall con-quer ev-'ry foe, And
long shall fame their names pro-claim, who fought at Wa-ter loo.

    G           C        Am  D7  G
At ten o'clock on Sunday, the bloody fight began,
D7  G             Am G  A7   D A7  D
It raged from that moment to the setting of the sun;
D7  G             G7  C E7 A7        D
My pen, I'm sure, can't half relate the glories of that day.
D7  G         C        Am   D7  G
We fought the French at Waterloo, and made them run away.

    G           C        Am  D7  G
On the eighteenth of June, eighteen-hundred-and-fifteen,
D7  G             Am  G    A7   D A7 D
Both horse and foot they did advance, most glorious to be seen,
D7  G             G7  C  E7   A7
Both horse and foot they did advance, and the bugle horn did
  D
 blow,
D7  G         C            Am
The sons of France we made them dance, on the plains of
  D7  G
 Waterloo.

    G           C        Am  D7  G
Our cavalry advanced with true and valiant hearts,
D7  G             Am G A7   D  A7   D
Our infantry and artillery did nobly play their parts;
D7  G             G7 C E7 A7            D
While the small arms did rattle and the great guns they did roar,
D7  G         C        Am  D7  G
And many a valiant soldier lay bleeding in his gore.

    G           C        Am  D7  G
The French dogs made a bold attack in front of Mount St. Jean,
D7  G             Am  G A7 D A7 D
Two of their best battalions thought the village to gain;
D7  G             G7     C E7 A7        D
Our infantry first charged them and made them face about,
D7  G         C        Am  D7  G
Sir William with his heavy brigade soon put them to the rout.

    G           C        Am D7 G
As for Sir William Ponsonby, I'm sorry for to say,
D7  G             Am  G A7   D  A7  D
Leading the Enniskillen dragoons, he met his fate that day;
D7  G             G7     C  E7  A7       D
In front of his brigade he fell, which grieves me very sore,
D7 G          C        Am  D7      G
I saw him lie as I passed by, with many thousands more.

    G           C        Am D7      G
The cuirassiers so nobly fought, armed in coats of steel,
D7  G             Am  G A7   D A7 D
And boldly they did advance, thinking to make us yield;
D7  G             G7    C  E7 A7
But our dragoons with sword in hand soon cut their armour
   D
 through,
D7  G             C        Am  D7      G
And showed that day at Waterloo, what Britons they could do.

```
     G           C            Am    D7 G
Napoleon, like a fighting cock, far mounted on a car,
D7 G              Am    G   A7      D  A7 D
He much did wish to represent great Mars the god of war;
D7 G           G7    C  E7 A7        D
On a high platform he did stand and loudly he did crow,
D7 G                    C           Am    D7 G
He dropt his wings and turned his tail to us at Waterloo.

     G           C          Am      D7      G
The fertile field of Brabant shall long recorded be,
 D7    G                Am G A7    D A7 D
Where Britons fought for honour  and  Belgic  liberty,
D7 G                 G7    C  E7 A7          D
The Sovereign of the Netherlands, he very well does know,
D7 G              C         Am       D7  G
For honour and his country, we fought at Waterloo.

     G              C           Am     D7       G
The Prince of Orange the hussars and right wing did command,
 D7  G                   Am G A7    D  A7 D
And sure a Prince more valiant ne'er took a sword in hand;
D7 G              G7     C  E7 A7         D
His Highness wounded was that day, charging the haughty foe,
D7 G              C             Am    D7     G
And long shall fame their name proclaim, who fought at Waterloo.

    G            C        Am      D7      G
The valiant Duke of Brunswick fell in the field that day,
D7 G         Am   G  A7         D
And many a valiant officer dropt in the awful fray,
D7 G       G7 C  E7  A7          D
And many British soldiers lay bleeding in their gore,
D7    G         C       Am       D7      G
On the plains of Waterloo, where thundering cannons roar.

     G            C         Am     D7        G
Lord Wellington commanded us all on the glorious day,
 D7   G          Am G  A7       D  A7 D
Where many a brave soldier in death's cold arms did lay;
 D7   G          G7  C E7 A7            D
Where many arms did rattle, and cannons loud did roar,
D7  G           C          Am D7    G
At Waterloo, where Frenchmen their fate did deplore.

 G        C       Am     D7   G
As for General Paget, Marquis of Anglesea,
 D7       G           Am  G A7     D A7 D
The commander of the brigade of British cavalry,
D7  G            G7      C   E7 A7       D
His honour most conspicuous shone wherever he did go,
D7 G            C            Am  D7    G
A limb he lost in a gallant charge that day at Waterloo.

      G            C              Am      D7
Brave General Hill, so much renowned, commanded the left
 G
 wing,
D7  G                   Am G  A7  D A7 D
And with his British hearts of oak, destruction did bring;
 D7   G          G7   C  E7  A7          D
Brave Picton of heroic fame his squadron on he drew,
 D7  G              C        Am     D7     G
Where all sublime his deeds do shine in fame at Waterloo.

      G              C            Am    D7       G
Now, tender husbands here have left their wives for to mourn,
D7  G             Am  G  A7      D A7 D
And children, weeping, cry, "When will our dads return?"
D7  G              G7      C  E7 A7           D
Our country will dry up their tears, we feel rejoiced to know,
 D7  G              C         Am   D7      G
They will reward each soldier that fought at Waterloo.

      G              C          Am       D7    G
When Bonaparte he did perceive the victory we had won,
D7 G             Am  G    A7      D A7 D
He did lament in bitter tears, saying "Oh! my darling son,
D7 G           G7    C  E7 A7               D
I will set off to Paris straight, and have him crowned also,
D7 G              C            Am    D7    G
Before they hear of my defeat on the plains of Waterloo."

     G             C          D7          G
So unto George, our gracious King, my voice I mean to raise,
D7 G                 Am  G A7     D  A7  D
And to all gallant commanders I wish to sing their praise;
D7  G               G7 C E7 A7          D
The Duke of York and family, and Wellington also,
 D7       G                C          Am
And the soldiers brave that fought that day on the plains of
 D7  G
 Waterloo.

     G            C         Am      D7     G
So let us give our praise to God, who did the victory give,
D7 G                Am  G A7         D
And may we all remember Him as long as we do live;
D7 G            G7      C  E7 A7              D
To God above give all the praise, and we'll remember, too,
D7    G           C           Am   D7   G
That He gave to us the victory on the plains of Waterloo.
```

# The Halcyon Days of Old England

Whig satirists did not hesitate to criticize the ineptitude of the Tory government during the American Revolutionary War. This appeared in the *London Evening Post* in 1778.

Let us laugh at the cavils of weak, silly elves;
      B7      C#m      F#7      B7
Our statesmen are wise men—they say so themselves.
      A            E        B
And though little mortals may hear it with wonder,
               F#7      B      B7
'Tis consummate wisdom that causes each blunder!   *Chorus*

             E            A     E
They are now engaged in a glorious war,
      B7      C#m      F#7      B7
It began about tea, about feathers and tar;
      A            E        B
With spirit they push what they've planned with sense,
               F#7      B      B7
Forty millions they've spent—for a tax of three pence! *Chorus*

             E            A      E
The debts of the nation do grieve them so sore,
      B7      C#m      F#7      B7
To lighten our burden, they load us the more!
      A            E        B
They aim at th' Americans' cash, my dear honey,
               F#7      B      B7
Yet beggar this kingdom and send them the money.   *Chorus*

```
           E                          A           E
What honors we're gaining by taking their forts,
    B7          C#m         F#7        B7
Destroying bateaux and blocking up ports!
    A                            E          B
Burgoyne would have worked 'em but for a mishap,
                        F#7        B        B7
By Gates and one Arnold, he's caught in a trap!        Chorus


           E                          A           E
But Howe was more cautious and prudent by far,
    B7          C#m         F#7        B7
He sailed with his fleet up the great Delaware;
    A                            E          B
All summer he struggled and strove to undo 'em,
                        F#7        B        B7
But the plague of it was, he could not get to them.    Chorus


           E                          A           E
Oh! think us not cruel, because our allies
    B7          C#m         F#7        B7
Are savagely scalping men, women and boys!
    A                            E          B
Maternal affection to this step doth move us,
                        F#7        B        B7
The more they are scalped, the more they will love us!  Chorus


           E                          A           E
Some folks are uneasy and make a great pother
    B7          C#m         F#7        B7
For the loss of one army and half of another;
    A                            E          B
But, sirs, next campaign by ten thousands we'll slay 'em
                     F#7        B        B7
If we can find soldiers—and money to pay 'em!          Chorus


           E                          A           E
I've sung you a song, now I'll give you a prayer;
    B7          C#m         F#7        B7
May peace soon succeed to this horrible war!
    A                            E          B
Again may we live with our brethren in concord,
                        F#7        B        B7
And the authors of mischief all hang on a strong cord.  Chorus
```

# Join the British Army

A barrack-room favorite since Victorian days.

When I was young I used to be as fine a man as you could see. The
Prince of Wales, he said to me, "Come join the Brit-ish ar-my."

*Chorus*
Too - ra-loo ra - loo ra-loo, They're look-ing for mon-keys in the zoo, And
if I had a face like you, I'd join the Brit-ish ar - my.

Dm
Sarah Comden baked a cake,
    Am        C
'Twas all for Corporal Slattery's sake.
Dm         F
I threw meself into the lake,
Gm        A7
Pretendin' I was barmy.

           Dm      Am
*Chorus:* Too-ra-loo-ra loo-ra-loo,
              F      C
       'Twas the only thing that I could do
       Dm
       To work me ticket home to you,
       A7          Dm
       And leave the British army.

Dm
Sergeant Daly's gone away,
    Am        C
His wife is in the family way.
Dm        F
The only thing that she can say
Gm        A7
Is, "Blame the British army!"

           Dm
*Chorus:* Too-ra-loo-ra loo-ra-loo,
              Am      F
       Me curses on the Labor crew.
       Dm         F
       They took your darlin' boy from you
       A7         Dm
       To join the British army.

Dm
Captain Duff's got such a drought,
    Am        C
Just give him a couple of jars of stout,
        Dm       F
And he'll beat the enemy with his mouth,
        Gm       A7
And save the British army.   *Chorus I*

Dm
Kilted soldiers wear no drawers,
    Am        C
Won't you kindly lend them yours?
    Dm          F
The poor should always help the poor—
        Gm       A7
God help the British army!   *Chorus I*

*Irish soldiers' verse*
          Dm
They'll beat the Germans without fuss
    Am        C
And lay their bones out in the dust.
Dm        F
I know, for they damn near beat us,
    Gm       A7
The gallant British army.

                 Dm
*Chorus:* Too-ra-loo-ra loo-ra-loo,
                 Am      C
          I've made me mind up what to do:
          Dm       F
          I'll work me ticket home to you,
          A7        Dm
          And leave the British army.

*Repeat first verse and chorus*

# Tell Me Boys, Have You Any Complaints?

Army food . . . the food you love to hate. The refrain refers to the practice of having an orderly officer visit each company at mess for the purpose of taking complaints about the quality of the food.

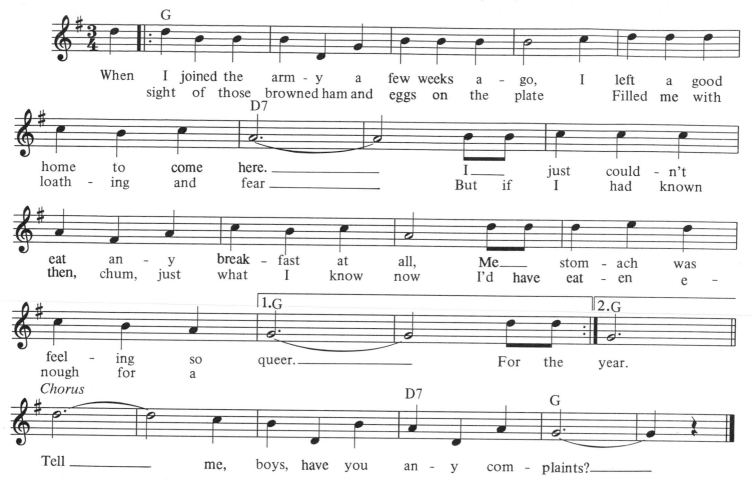

When I joined the arm-y a few weeks a-go, I left a good
sight of those browned ham and eggs on the plate Filled me with

home to come here. ____ I ____ just could-n't
loath-ing and fear ____ But if I had known

eat an-y break-fast at all, Me ____ stom-ach was
then, chum, just what I know now I'd have eat-en e-

1.G
feel-ing so queer. ____ For the year.
nough for a

2.G

*Chorus*

Tell ____ me, boys, have you an-y com-plaints? ____

G
The very next morning they bunged us some fish,

D7
And, believe me, boys, that fish was cute,

For that so-and-so fish it stood up in the dish
G
And it gave us the fascist salute.

Well, the fellows turned pale as they rose from their seats,

D7
Some of them more than half dead.

You can take it from me that the war would have stopped,
G
If they'd given it the Nazis instead. *Chorus*

G
Every Monday for dinner they give us brown stew,

D7
And on Tuesday as well for a treat.

We get stew so often, chum, that we thank God
G
That there's only seven days in a week.

For the duffs are now brown, and the stew is brown stew,

D7
They're all fancy names for the scoff.

It would be for more honest to say that brown stew
D
Was stew that was bloody browned-off. *Chorus*